TEACHING Social Skills to Youth with Mental Health DISORDERS

Also from the Boys Town Press

Teaching Social Skills to Youth
Basic Social Skills for Youth
Changing Children's Behavior by Changing the People,
    Places, and Activities in Their Lives
Tools for Teaching Social Skills in School
More Tools for Teaching Social Skills in School
No Room for Bullies
Skills for Families, Skills for Life
Building Skills in High-Risk Families
Rebuilding Children's Lives
Effective Skills for Child-Care Workers
Common Sense Parenting®
Common Sense Parenting DVD Series
Parenting to Build Character in Your Teen
Common Sense Parenting of Toddlers and Preschoolers
The Well-Managed Classroom
Effective Study Strategies for Every Classroom
Practical Tools for Foster Parents
Who's Raising Your Child?
Good Night, Sweet Dreams, I Love You:
    Now Get into Bed and Go to Sleep
There Are No Simple Rules for Dating My Daughter
Unmasking Sexual Con Games
Fathers, Come Home

For Adolescents
Boundaries: A Guide for Teens
A Good Friend
Who's in the Mirror?
What's Right for Me?
Little Sisters, Listen Up
Guys, Let's Keep It Real

For more information, visit our Web site:
www.boystownpress.org

Boys Town National Hotline
1-800-448-3000
A crisis, resource and referral number especially for kids and parents.

TEACHING Social Skills to Youth with Mental Health DISORDERS

Incorporating Social Skills into Treatment Planning *for* 109 Disorders

JENNIFER RESETAR VOLZ, PH.D.

TARA SNYDER, PSY.D.

MICHAEL STERBA, M.H.D.

BOYS TOWN Press

Boys Town, Nebraska

Teaching Social Skills to Youth with Mental Health Disorders

Published by the Boys Town Press
14100 Crawford St.
Boys Town, Nebraska 68010

Copyright © 2009, Father Flanagan's Boys' Home

ISBN 978-1-934490-10-5

Boys Town Press is the publishing division of Boys Town, a national organization serving children and families.

Publisher's Cataloging in Publication

Volz, Jennifer Resetar.
    Teaching social skills to youth with mental health disorders : incorporating social skills into treatment planning for 109 disorders / Jennifer Resetar Volz, Tara Snyder, Michael Sterba. -- 1st ed. -- Boys Town, Neb. : Boys Town Press, c2009.

        p. ; cm.
        ISBN: 978-1-934490-10-5
        Includes bibliographical references and index.

        1. Child psychotherapy. 2. Adolescent psychotherapy. 3. Social skills in children--Study and teaching. 4. Mentally ill children--Care. 5. Developmentally disabled children--Care. I. Snyder, Tara. II. Sterba, Michael. III. Title.

RJ499 .V65 2009
618.92/89--dc22   0901

15 14 13 12 11 10 9 8 7 6 5 4 3 2 1

Acknowledgments

This book would not have been possible without the commitment and ongoing efforts of many people. We would like to thank the following people for their contributions: Lisa Batenhorst, Dr. Dan Daly, Cathy DeSalvo, Tom Dowd, Dr. Pat Friman, Gary Feller, Jim Gross, Terry Hyland, Lynn Ingraham, Jay Ringle, Dr. Ron Thompson, and Dennis Volmer.

Table of Contents

Introduction 1

Chapter 1
Psychological Assessment and the DSM-IV-TR. . . . 9

Chapter 2
Individualizing Treatment Plans 17

Chapter 3
Social Skills and Mental Health Disorders 29

Chapter 4
Social Skill Charts for Specific
Mental Health Disorders 43

Chapter 5
Treatment Planning with a Focus on
Social Skill Instruction. 129

Appendix
Basic Social Skills and Their Steps 171

References 175

Index 179

Introduction

"Hyper" Harry

Harry, an eleven-year-old boy, is described by his parents and teachers as a child whose "motor is always running." It's been that way since Harry entered kindergarten at age five. In the classroom, it is difficult for Harry to pay or sustain attention; he doesn't concentrate on details and, as a result, makes careless mistakes in his schoolwork. Harry's teachers frequently reprimand him for interrupting others, not waiting his turn, and constantly talking to other classmates during study time, even when the students are given time to quietly do something they like. He regularly loses his homework and textbooks or forgets to bring them home, and when he does remember, his parents report "it's like pulling teeth" to get him to sit down for any length of time to complete his studies. As a result, his grades are failing, even though his teachers say he's capable of doing the work.

At home, it is more of the same. Harry forgets to do chores and has trouble sitting through dinner and other family activities. Harry's father thinks Harry is "lazy" and "irresponsible" and that he would do better in school and at home if he just "applied himself and tried harder." Lately, Harry and his father have had heated arguments over Harry's failing schoolwork and his forgetfulness regarding his chores. Harry's relationships with his parents, brother and sisters, teachers, and friends are becoming strained, causing Harry further frustration and resulting in more frequent temper outbursts.

Recently, Harry was referred by his teacher for a full psychoeducational evaluation. Because Harry's symptoms are seriously affecting his academic and social functioning at school, it was determined that he qualified for special education services under the category "Other Health Impairment (OHI)." Harry's parents agreed that his symptoms also are causing significant problems at home. The school psychologist provided Harry's parents with phone numbers of several local counselors. Harry's parents took him to counseling, and, after several sessions, it became clear to Harry's therapist that the family needed extra support in managing Harry's behavior. Harry's therapist recommended that they contact family preservation services.

"Unmanageable" Dwayne

Over the past year, Dwayne's temper has gotten worse. He frequently "loses his cool" when his mother asks him to help out at home or do his chores. At these times, Dwayne argues and often gets into shouting matches with his mother; he curses, openly tests her authority, and is verbally aggressive. Dwayne's mother describes her twelve-year-old son as stubborn and unwilling to compromise or negotiate with her. She says, "He wants it his way or no way." Many times, Dwayne refuses his mother's requests by simply ignoring her and purposely breaks the rules she makes. Dwayne's mother tries to discipline her son by grounding him or not letting him watch TV or talk on the phone, but he doesn't accept the consequences. He won't take responsibility for his behavior and constantly makes up stories and lies or blames others for his misdeeds.

These same behaviors are becoming more and more prevalent at school. His teachers are frustrated by his constant challenges to their authority, rules, and consequences. Dwayne is spending more time in the office for his defiance, and his schoolwork is suffering. When Dwayne is in class, his teachers report that he deliberately annoys other students and is spiteful and vindictive toward classmates and teachers whom he believes "have done him wrong."

Recently, Dwayne was kicked out of the local mall by a security officer after the officer questioned him and a friend about a shoplifting incident that neither boy was involved in. During the questioning, Dwayne got mad and threatened the security guard. Dwayne doesn't have many friends anymore, and his mother considers the friends that he does have to be "troublemakers." Dwayne and his mother have been attending outpatient therapy for the past six months with no real results. During therapy sessions, Dwayne is defensive and, at times, refuses to talk to his therapist. During the most recent session, Dwayne's therapist suggested that a higher level of care may be necessary. Dwayne's mother, at the end her rope, made the decision to place him in a residential group home program.

"Down in the Dumps" Jamie

Twice during the past year, thirteen-year-old Jamie tried to commit suicide. On both occasions, she was briefly hospitalized in an inpatient care facility. The first attempt was ten months ago when Jamie overdosed on aspirin; recently, she cut her wrists. She says she tried to hurt herself because she is "no good" and "doesn't care more."

During the last year and a half, Jamie has been "down in the dumps" several times. During these stretches, which often last a few weeks, her parents report that Jamie has no energy and constantly seems tired and fatigued; they often find her tearful and crying. It is almost impossible to get her to go to school, where she previously had been a good student and active in school activities and sports. Once an "A" and "B" student, her grades have dropped dramatically, and she is currently failing most of her classes. Jamie's teachers are concerned; they report she has difficulty concentrating, is easily distracted, and is unable to make simple decisions like what topic to select for an English paper. Most surprisingly, Jamie doesn't have any interest in going to drama practice. She usually loves this activity and has been in many plays since she was very young. Three months ago, when she wasn't in one of her "down cycles," she earned a major role in the school play; now she wants to quit. Jamie says she is no good and would only "screw it up."

At meals, Jamie just picks at her favorite foods. She is a slim girl, so her weight loss is noticeable. Jamie says that it is difficult for her to get to sleep. She also reports she wakes up in the middle of the night and can't get back to sleep. During the day, she is irritable and spends most of her time alone in her room. Her friends call and ask her to go out but she says she is too tired. Her parents are afraid she might succeed in hurting herself; they "want the old Jamie back."

Since Jamie's first suicide attempt, she has been attending both outpatient therapy and psychiatric visits regularly. During the most recent session with her psychologist, Jamie reported active suicidal ideation. She had a plan and meant to carry it out. Jamie also admitted to cutting her inner thighs with a razor blade several times a week to "punish herself." Jamie's psychologist provided Jamie's psychiatrist with this information, and the psychiatrist recommended placement in an intensive residential psychiatric program for youth.

Mental Health Disorder Diagnoses

Each of the youths described in these three examples is suffering from a mental health disorder. Harry's behaviors and related symptoms point to Attention-Deficit/Hyperactivity Disorder. The temper outbursts and aggression displayed by Dwayne could be signs of Oppositional Defiant Disorder. Finally, Jamie's attempts to harm herself indicate Major Depressive Disorder.

These types of diagnoses are defined by the *Diagnostic and Statistical Manual of Mental Disorders, Fourth Edition, Text Revision* (DSM-IV-TR), one of the world's standard tools for evaluating and diagnosing mental health disorders in children, adolescents, and adults. Progress in classifying and identifying mental health disorders has led to improved instruction and training for treatment providers that is more intensely focused on how to effectively treat youth with specific mental health disorders. This, in turn, has led to more appropriate and accurate treatment for youth.

Helping caregivers and treatment providers further improve the care they provide is the goal of this book. Through years of experience working with thousands of children and adolescents with behavioral and mental disorders, Boys Town's research has proven that social skill instruction – teaching youth alternative positive behaviors they can use to replace current inappropriate behavior – is extremely effective in helping youth overcome their problems. In many situations, a lack of certain social skills can contribute to, and often exacerbate, an existing mental health disorder. For example, if Harry were to learn skills such as "Following Instructions" or "Staying on Task," and these were reinforced both at school and at home, some of his problem behaviors would improve, alleviating many of the frustrations related to Harry's behaviors.

By showing how this social skill instruction approach can be applied to the treatment of DSM-IV-TR disorders, this book can serve as a valuable guide in helping treatment providers effectively and successfully treat youth in their care. (Treatment providers can include youth-care workers, group home caregivers, consultants, foster parents, shelter workers and administrators, family interventionists, staff working in psychiatric settings, teachers, school counselors, therapists, social workers, psychiatrists, physicians, psychologists, clinicians, and other health and mental health professionals.)

What's in This Book

There are five parts to this book. A history of the DSM-IV-TR is outlined in the first chapter, along with an introduction to the importance of other mental health disorder assessment and evaluation tools. There also is an explanation of the multiaxial assessment system – detailed in the DSM-IV-TR – that can help mental health professionals during the evaluation process. A discussion of individualized treatment planning regarding DSM-IV-TR mental health disorder diagnoses and social skill instruction follows in the second chapter.

The third chapter discusses the Boys Town Teaching Model, the Boys Town Social Skill Curriculum, the concept of social skill instruction, and the importance and effectiveness of such teaching in the treatment of mental health disorders.

Chapter 4 offers a series of charts containing DSM-IV-TR diagnoses that are common for children and adolescents, and the various social skills that caregivers and treatment providers might target as part of a treatment plan for each disorder. These charts don't include all DSM-IV-TR disorders, but those that are likely to have associated social skills deficits that might be targeted in treatment. The various disorders and charts are listed in the order they appear in the DSM-IV-TR.

Examples of treatment plans for the three youth described at the beginning of this book are included in Chapter 5. These examples demonstrate how social skills can be integrated into a youth's overall treatment plan for particular DSM-IV-TR diagnoses across different settings – home and school, residential group home, and psychiatric facility – and levels of care.

Of course, only qualified professionals who have had the proper schooling, clinical training, and experience should use the DSM-IV-TR to evaluate and diagnose youth who may have a mental health disorder. This book is intended only as a guide for how to integrate social skill training into treatment planning and should not be used to make diagnoses. (Youth will see a therapist, psychologist, or psychiatrist for assessment and diagnostic purposes. An accurate DSM-IV-TR diagnosis of a troubled youth enables treatment providers across the entire spectrum of treatment settings – home, schools, shelters, foster care, residential treatment programs, psychiatric treatment settings, and so on – to develop better, more effective treatment plans.)

We hope you find this book useful in your work with children and adolescents. All youth must learn social skills in order to find success in their lives. Teaching these social skills as part of treatment for a mental health disorder truly can enhance a youth's progress and help him or her to overcome problems.

About the Authors

Dr. Jennifer Resetar Volz is a licensed psychologist at the Boys Town Behavioral Pediatrics and Family Services Outpatient Clinic. She received her doctoral degree from Louisiana State University in Baton Rouge, Louisiana. She is a nationally certified school psychologist as well as a board certified behavior analyst.

Dr. Tara Snyder is a provisionally licensed psychologist and licensed mental health professional at the Boys Town Behavioral Pediatrics and Family Services Outpatient Clinic. She received her doctoral degree in clinical psychology from Midwestern University in Downers Grove, Illinois.

Michael Sterba is a Senior Writer at Boys Town and is the co-author of numerous books for youth-care professionals. He received a Master of Human Development degree from the University of Kansas in Lawrence, Kansas.

Chapter 1

Psychological Assessment and the DSM-IV-TR

The initial impetus for developing a classification of mental health disorders was the collection of statistical information for the U.S. Census back in 1840. At that time, there was one crude category for such disorders – "idiocy/insanity." By the 1880 census, there were seven categories of mental illnesses. This gathering of statistical information on mental health disorders continued until 1952. That's when the first edition of the *Diagnostic and Statistical Manual of Mental Disorders* (or DSM-I) was published by the American Psychiatric Association. This manual contained a glossary of descriptions of the diagnostic categories and was the first official manual of mental health disorders designed for clinical use. Shortly thereafter, the DSM-II, which contained a new round of diagnostic revisions, was published. The DSM-III followed in 1980. It introduced a number of important methodological innovations and a descriptive approach that attempted to be neutral with respect to the theories of etiology. In 1987, the American Psychiatric Association published the DSM-III-R, which contained revisions and corrections for inconsistencies and instances where criteria were not entirely clear in the DSM-III (American Psychiatric Association, 1994).

The DSM-IV, published in 1994, came about due to the substantial increase in research that was generated by the DSM-III and DSM-III-R. By that time, research regarding diagnoses was available in the empirical literature or other data sets. The DSM-IV content was based on "...historical tradition (as embodied in the DSM-III and DSM-III-R)..., evidence from reviews of the literature, analyses of unpublished data sets, results of field trials, and consensus of the field" (American Psychiatric Association, 2000, p. xxvii). The DSM-IV includes 340 mental health disorders, nearly 120 more than the DSM-III-R. In 2000, the DSM-IV-TR was released in order to address necessary text revisions. There were no major changes to diagnostic criteria, and no diagnoses were added or removed; the revisions were mainly to correct errors and provide updates.

The Use of Multiaxial Assessment

In order to arrive at an accurate DSM-IV-TR diagnosis, and ultimately provide successful treatment, an effective evaluation process is necessary. One widely recognized procedure for evaluating an individual with a mental health disorder is the multiaxial assessment system detailed in the DSM-IV-TR. In this process, mental health professionals obtain comprehensive information about different domains in a person's life and then examine this information during the evaluation process to help them achieve the most precise DSM-IV-TR disorder diagnosis possible.

The DSM-IV multiaxial assessment system includes:

Axis I	Clinical Disorders
	Other Conditions That May Be a Focus of Clinical Attention
Axis II	Personality Disorders
	Mental Retardation
Axis III	General Medical Conditions
Axis IV	Psychosocial and Environmental Problems
Axis V	Global Assessment of Functioning

Axis I and Axis II are two separate classifications that contain all the various mental health disorders in the DSM-IV-TR. The items grouped and reported under Axis I are classified by the DSM-IV-TR as "Clinical Disorders" or "Other Conditions That May Be a Focus of Clinical Attention," while the disorders grouped and reported under Axis II are classified by the DSM-IV-TR as "Personality Disorders" or "Mental Retardation." The reason for separating these two less common categories of disorders into different axes is to ensure that they will be given adequate consideration by mental health professionals and not be overlooked due to a focus on the more common clinical disorders listed in Axis I.

The focus of Axis III is any current general medical conditions that might be relevant to the understanding or management of an individual's mental health disorder. An example of this, according to the DSM-IV-TR, would be when "...hypothyroidism is a direct cause of depressive symptoms..." (American Psychiatric Association, 2000, p. 29). The DSM-IV-TR says that "Axis IV is for reporting psychosocial and environmental problems that may affect diagnosis, treatment, and prognosis..." (American Psychiatric Association, 2000, p. 31) of a DSM-IV-TR disorder. Examples of this include divorce, death of a family member, job loss, being a crime victim, and so on. Mental health professionals also are asked to report the severity (mild, moderate, or severe) of the present stressors.

Finally, Axis V summarizes a mental health professional's judgment of an individual's overall level of functioning on the Global Assessment of Functioning (GAF) scale. The GAF scale can be used at admission, at various times during treatment, and at discharge. Using this scale can be extremely beneficial in treatment planning and in measuring the success of treatment over time.

According to the DSM-IV-TR, "a multiaxial system provides a convenient format for organizing and communicating clinical information, for capturing the complexity of clinical situations, and for describing the heterogeneity of individuals presenting with the same diagnosis. In addition, the multiaxial system promotes the application of the biopsychosocial approach model in clinical, educational, and research settings" (American Psychiatric Association, 2000, p. 27). Such a comprehensive and systematic evaluation system allows a mental health professional to take into account all aspects of a person's life that might be contributing to the problem instead of focusing only on a single presenting problem. In the end, this extensive evaluation process greatly enhances a mental health professional's diagnostic capabilities.

DSM-IV-TR and Diagnostic Assessment

The DSM-IV-TR is generally one of the first evaluation tools utilized by trained and knowledgeable mental health professionals to accurately diagnose mental health disorders. Other information can come from youth interviews, parent/guardian interviews, teacher interviews, medical records, educational records, educational assessments, psychological assessments, behavioral observations, and other measures. The use of these methods allows mental health professionals to gather more detailed information about a youth's problem, thus helping to strengthen the accuracy of the evaluation and diagnostic process.

Another important evaluation tool widely used by mental health professionals – in concert with the DSM-IV-TR – is the National Institute of Mental Health Diagnostic Interview Schedule for Children (DISC) (Shaffer, Fisher, & Lucas, 1997). This is a structured interview for children and adolescents that allows mental health professionals to obtain diagnostic criteria information for common psychiatric disorders. Friman (1997) says that DISC data "...provides information on the kinds of psychological problems exhibited by youth..." entering various treatment environments and that "the value of this information is most apparent in treatment planning" (p. 192).

Psychological assessments are often used by mental health professionals when considering diagnosis. Behavior rating report forms are simple psychological assessment tools designed to produce valid diagnostic information. Several assessment systems utilize multi-informant report rating scales. Some of these include:

- Achenbach System for Empirically Based Assessment (ASEBA) – Child Behavior Checklist Parent Form (CBCL), Achenbach Teacher Report Form (TRF), and Achenbach Youth Self-Report Form (YSRF) (Achenbach & Rescorla, 2001)

- Behavior Assessment System for Children, Second Edition (BASC-2) – Parent Rating Scales (PRS), Teacher Rating Scales (TRS), and Self-Report of Personality (SRP) (Reynolds & Kamphaus, 2004)

- Conners' Comprehensive Behavior Rating Scales (CBRS) – Parent Response Booklet (P), Teacher Response Booklet (T), and Self-Report Response Booklet (SR) (Conners, 2008)

These assessment tools produce a variety of information about a youth's perceived behavioral, emotional, and social functioning. The system utilized will depend on a youth's age, available informants, and the specific information that is desired. Scores on these assessments can help to indicate whether or not a youth is experiencing more symptoms than most youth his or her age and gender. This information also can be helpful when planning and evaluating treatment plans for particular youth.

Educational assessments also are used by mental health professionals and school personnel to provide information about a youth's cognitive ability or achievement. These scores are important to consider when developing treatment plans. For example, if a youth's verbal ability is significantly below average, a treatment strategy that relies heavily on language would not be appropriate for that youth.

Cognitive ability provides information about an individual's capabilities in a variety of areas (verbal comprehension, perceptual reasoning, processing speed, working memory, etc.) and is often termed an individual's intelligence quotient or "IQ." There are numerous tests that measure IQ; each differs in the appropriate age range for testing and the specific domains of intelligence that are considered. Some common examples include:

- Weschler Preschool and Primary Scale of Intelligence, Third Edition (WPPSI-III) (Weschler, 2002a)
- Weschler Intelligence Scale for Children, Fourth Edition (WISC-IV) (Weschler, 2003)
- Weschler Adult Intelligence Scale, Third Edition (WAIS-III) (Weschler, 1997)
- Weschler Abbreviated Scale of Intelligence (WASI) (Weschler, 1999)
- Stanford-Binet Intelligence Scale, Fifth Edition (SB5) (Roid, 2003)
- Woodcock-Johnson III Tests of Cognitive Abilities (WJ-III) (Woodcock, McGrew, & Mather, 2001a).

Achievement is the level at which an individual is currently performing in a given academic area (reading, mathematics, written language, oral language, etc.). Achievement scores are used to determine whether or not an individual meets criteria for a learning disability. Generally, a large discrepancy between one's ability and one's achievement indicates that a learning disability may be present, since the individual is not achieving at the level that would be expected.

Like ability measures, there are many available achievement measures that test a variety of academic areas. Examples include:

- Weschler Individual Achievement Test, Second Edition (WIAT-II) (Weschler, 2002b)
- Woodcock Johnson III Tests of Achievement (WJ-III) (Woodcock, McGrew, & Mather, 2001b)
- Wide Range Achievement Test, Fourth Edition (WRAT-4) (Wilkinson & Robertson, 2005)

Many types of assessment methods can be used to help mental health professionals arrive at an appropriate diagnosis. These methods also can be helpful when developing treatment plans and evaluating the effectiveness of interventions. Only a handful of assessment measures were selected for this discussion; numerous others are frequently used.

Summary

The DSM-IV-TR evolved from a mere collection of statistical information for the U.S. Census in 1840 to being the world's standard tool for evaluating and diagnosing mental health disorders in children, adolescents, and adults. Numerous assessment tools have been devised to help in diagnosis determination. A few of these measures include the DISC, behavior rating report forms, cognitive tests, and achievement tests. Besides providing mental health professionals with more comprehensive information during the evaluation process, these tools also help produce thorough evaluations that lead to more accurate diagnoses. This information enables treatment providers to create and develop therapeutic, successful treatment plans for youth who require mental health services.

Chapter 2

Individualizing Treatment Plans

In order to develop effective and successful treatment plans for youth, treatment providers must take into account the many individual factors that make up a young person's life. There are developmental, cultural, behavioral, emotional, social, genetic, and biological variables that are unique to each person. In addition to social skill deficits, individualized treatment plans require the consideration of all the components currently affecting the youth. This helps treatment providers to achieve optimal treatment goals with each youth in their care. This chapter presents brief discussions on several of the variables previously listed and provides examples of how they can be incorporated into social skill treatment planning.

Developmental Considerations

A youth's developmental level plays a huge role in constructing an appropriate treatment plan. Knowledge of typical development provides an idea of when particular skills generally emerge, what skills are most appropriate to target, and the best way to teach skills. Many theories have been devised to describe development in multiple areas, including cognition, morals, identity, language, socioemotional, social, psychosexual, and attachment. (For detailed information on any of the above theories, see a developmental text such as, *A Child's World: Infancy Through Adolescence,* by Papalia, Olds, & Feldman, 2005). In this section, we will highlight how to consider development when planning social skill instruction.

Treatment providers must consider a youth's developmental level when determining whether a social skill deficit exists. For example, children in early childhood are known for fairly egocentric thought – thinking that others' experiences are similar to their own. When this is the case, children, given their developmental level, would not be expected to be able to identify how their actions affect others. By late childhood and early adolescence, however, this skill should be acquired, so an absence of empathy might be seen as a social skill deficit. A youth's developmental level will dictate whether the absence of a skill is an indication of abnormal development or an age-appropriate deficit.

Developmental level also will guide what skills to target for treatment. In Chapter 4, "Suggested Social Skill Training for Individuals Diagnosed with Mental Health Disorders," skills are listed in order from "basic" to "complex." Some of the more complex skills ("Budgeting and Managing Money," "Using Strategies to Find a Job," etc.) will not be appropriate for younger girls and boys. In addition, children should master basic skills before intermediate skills are taught, intermediate skills should be learned prior to training in advanced skills, and so on. Therefore, you may have to delay teaching some of the skills suggested for particular mental health disorders until a youth masters other targeted basic skills. For example, a person would need to learn the skill of "Talking to Others" (basic skill) before he or she could learn the skill of "Contributing to Discussions" (complex skill). The main point to consider here is whether a targeted skill needs to build upon another more basic skill.

Finally, a youth's developmental level will play a role in how skills are taught. For example, the social skill instruction model used at Boys Town requires youth to have attained a certain level of language and cognitive development. Youth who possess low cognitive functioning and/or poor language skills would be better served by treatment programs that use less language-based teaching and more behaviorally based teaching. Youth who perform at lower cognitive ranges can benefit from social skill training taught through the Boys Town Teaching Model, but accommodations should be considered. In Boys Town residential homes, one such accommodation to the social skills model is a token economy system. This combines the social skill training model with a behavioral motivation system that helps produce optimal results. Learning occurs at both the verbal and behavioral level. Another possible accommodation for youth with lower cognitive functioning would include providing social skill cards that include steps and pictures that help youth learn the skills. Using these cards also could earn rewards for youth via a motivation system. Conversely, youth with average intellect may not necessarily require as many prompts and cues for learning to take place.

There are many forms of development to consider when creating individualized treatment plans. In this section, we briefly touched on development areas that should be considered when using the Boys Town Teaching Model, which is discussed later in this book. A youth's developmental level will ultimately guide treatment providers as they determine which skill deficit to address, what social skills to choose for instruction, and how best to teach these skills.

Cultural Considerations

The **ADDRESSING** framework is a tool that can help guide culturally responsive treatment methods that allow youth to grow. ADDRESSING is an acronym that stands for **A**ge and generational influences; **D**evelopmental and acquired **D**isabilities; **R**eligion and spiritual orientation; **E**thnicity; **S**ocioeconomic status; **S**exual orientation; **I**ndigenous heritage; **N**ational origin; and **G**ender. This tool can help treatment providers understand the important role culture plays in a youth's development and account for cultural groups and influences. The focus of this approach is to look at how each individual's multicultural background influences knowledge, skills, and attitudes about external and internal worlds. It is also essential that treatment providers develop cultural responsiveness, which begins with self-assessment of one's own culture and biases and continues with education about other cultures and beliefs (Hays, 2008).

When social skill instruction is part of an individualized treatment plan, cultural and ethnic factors will influence what skills are targeted, how these skills are taught, and what skill components are included. For example, many Native American cultures consider it a sign of disrespect for a youth to make direct eye contact with an adult. But, almost all of the social skills taught in the Boys Town Teaching Model include the component, "Look at the person." Therefore, when teaching this specific behavior to Native American youth, a treatment provider may need to modify or target it for extra teaching and shape it over a longer period of time. The provider also should teach discrimination skills to Native American youth, helping them to understand that it is acceptable to look at their teacher at school or boss at work, but may not be appropriate to make eye contact with elders in their own culture.

When teaching youth skills that are outside their comfort level or that go against cultural expectations, it is important that the individuals who are working with these youth understand and support them. Treatment providers should appreciate how a youth's culture has influenced his or her beliefs, behaviors, and values. More importantly, they should be comfortable with understanding their own cultural identities, values, and biases so that they can be more proactive and effective with the youth they are serving. When teaching youth social skills, treatment providers should evaluate how learning a new set of skills will affect how youth identify themselves, both inside and outside the treatment setting. As they feel accepted and develop a sense of belonging, some youth may begin to culturally identify with treatment providers and other youth within the treatment setting. But, if they feel that they are being forced to acculturate into the traditional American mainstream, they also might resist treatment.

Finally, culturally competent treatment providers should be aware that culture, race, and ethnicity are not to be used interchangeably since they each have a different meaning. Culture has shared elements, including language, history, and geographic location, but there is no biological link. For example, culture can be as broad as the Muslim religious communities in North America, which include people of African, Arab, Pakistani, East Indian, Middle Eastern, and African American descent.

Race is based on geography and physical characteristics (skin color, facial features, etc.) that tend to be genetically related. Race often is an aspect of an individual's self-identification, but it offers little information about the person. For example, race may identify one's social heritage but it clarifies little in terms of an individual's educational level, cultural context, or current environment. When formulating a treatment plan, knowledge of a youth's race can help treatment providers determine whether the youth considers himself or herself to be part of the dominant or minority culture and the impact that will have on treatment goals.

Ethnicity involves one's shared values and customs as well as beliefs, norms, behaviors, and institutions. Ethnicity also formulates many labels and perceptions that are not necessarily true for all members who may belong to the same ethnic group (Hays, 2008). So, for example, when treatment planning, one should not assume that all Native American youth have difficulty making eye contact with adults or that all Japanese or Korean youth group themselves within the "Asian" category.

It is important to be aware of how the traditional Eurocentric American culture and beliefs vary from those of other cultures. Society has set rules and norms for how individuals should think and behave. If a youth's behavior detours too far from these norms, it is possible that the youth meets criteria for a DSM-IV-TR diagnosis. Before making a diagnosis, it is important to consider symptoms, clarify how they may fit into the individual's culture, and determine if the symptoms are socially acceptable.

Behavioral and Emotional Considerations

Emotion and behavior are two crucial individual variables to take into account when developing individualized treatment plans. When working with youth with behavioral and/or emotional problems, specific treatment issues should be clearly defined and targeted. Some of these issues will likely include social skill deficits. But while many social skills deficits can potentially be a cause and/or effect of a mental health disorder, it is also important to address other aspects of behavioral and emotional problems when developing a thorough individualized treatment plan. It is likely that behavioral and emotional issues will become clear when referral concerns and symptoms are considered because they tend to be related.

One clear example of how individual behavioral and emotional considerations come into play can be seen by looking at youth who experience externalizing disorders versus internalizing disorders. Externalizing disorders include DSM-IV-TR diagnoses like Oppositional Defiant Disorder and Conduct Disorder, while internalizing disorders include diagnoses like Generalized Anxiety Disorder and Major Depressive Disorder. Youth diagnosed with externalizing disorders may be more likely to express themselves through their behaviors, while youth with internalizing disorders may be more likely to express themselves through language. This provides an indication of the best way to teach social skills to particular youth. For example, youth who are diagnosed with an externalizing disorder may respond better to short and direct instructions, while youth diagnosed with internalizing disorders may respond more readily to commands that include lengthy rationales and empathetic statements. Each youth is different, but identifying broad emotional and behavioral styles will help predict responses to different forms of instruction.

Another significant behavioral consideration is the youth's learning history. A learning history includes the behaviors that have been trained, shaped, reinforced, and punished. Understanding a youth's learning history will help those developing the treatment plan to better understand what goals need to be accomplished and how to best achieve those goals. Let's consider a thirteen-year-old youth whose entire life has consisted of variable attention (reinforcement) for arguing and being ignored (punishment) after making appropriate requests. It will take this youth much longer to learn the skill of "Accepting 'No' for an Answer" because of a learning history that has punished this behavior. It is important for treatment providers to keep those kinds of factors in mind when working with youth so they are able to set realistic time frames for treatment goals.

Obviously, some youth will have learning histories in which appropriate skills that are suggested for particular disorders have been reinforced. In these cases, there will not be a deficit of reinforced skills and they may not need to be taught and trained. These circumstances also should lead treatment providers to consider motivational deficits as a bigger reason for why youth are not displaying skills, and to address that in the individualized treatment plan.

Treatment providers also are encouraged to assess whether the behaviors and emotions associated with a youth's diagnosis serve a particular function in his or her life. Youth may exhibit particular behaviors in order to maintain relative stability within their home, gain attention from adults or peers, or get out of trouble or having to do something. Consider a boy diagnosed with Oppositional Defiant Disorder. A common symptom associated with this disorder is deliberately annoying others. A thorough assessment might reveal that the youth pinches his sister and swears at his mother for the purpose of gaining their attention, and that he enjoys the negative attention his sister and mother provide when they are upset. Not only will this youth need to be taught the social skill of "Getting Another Person's Attention," but his family also will need to be taught how to withhold negative attention when he uses annoying behaviors and offer positive attention when he appropriately seeks attention.

A youth's level of emotional development also comes into play when developing individualized treatment. Emotional expression is on a continuum, with some individuals being extremely emotional and others exhibiting no emotion. For example, individuals with

Asperger's Disorder tend to have a very limited emotional range and might seem to exhibit an overall "flat" affect. This is a disorder associated skill deficit that might require the treatment provider to work with the youth to identify and express his or her emotions before working on basic skills like "Showing Sensitivity to Others." Making eye contact, a step in most basic social skills, also will need to be shaped prior to working on specific social skills.

Other individuals may be on the opposite end of the continuum, where the intensity of emotion and the ease of arousal are issues. This might be the case for some youth who are diagnosed with Mood Disorders. For these youth, teaching a social skill like "Controlling Emotions" will be essential, and education on appropriate emotional expression, how emotional expression affects relationships, and what part medication plays in emotional regulation would be necessary adjuncts to an individualized treatment plan.

As we discussed, extreme emotions and behaviors are associated with many DSM-IV-TR diagnoses. Some aspects of emotion and behavior to consider include development, range, intensity, duration, frequency, form, function, cultural expectations, and history. A treatment plan that addresses all of these dimensions increases the likelihood that emotional and behavioral symptoms associated with a youth's diagnosis are treated.

Social Considerations

A youth's physical, emotional, and behavioral functioning can be greatly affected by ecological circumstances. These include, but are not limited to, family, school, peers, socioeconomic status, religion/church, and community. Social environment plays a large role in defining an individual, and provides a context for understanding an individual's past and current behavior. The impact of social factors cannot be overlooked when a treatment provider's goal is to devise a truly individualized treatment plan.

When assessing a youth and developing a treatment plan, the treatment provider should look for positive social variables as well as risk factors. For example, youth from lower-income families generally experience little power within systems they encounter, like education or health systems. Often, these youth witness their parents' frustrations and struggles, which can cause youth to feel helpless and insecure, as if external forces are controlling their lives. These types of social experiences can influence a youth's sense of security and trust, which in turn affects how they respond to treatment and those who provide it. This is one reason why older youth should be involved in the development of their treatment plans; it provides them with a sense of control and ownership.

Throughout a youth's development, individuals involved in his or her life (parents, teachers, peers, etc.) influence the youth's social growth through reinforcement, punishment, and modeling. Youth also acquire a wide breadth of social knowledge and responses by observing and imitating their parents', siblings', and peers' behaviors. This valuable information teaches youth social norms, rules, and ways to interact with others that may not always be prosocial but help them survive within their environment or get their physiological needs met. This is apparent when working with youth who have been involved in gangs. Typically, youth report that gang involvement provides prestige and safety within their community. Although this involvement is not desirable in mainstream society, some within the youth's community may view it as a protective mechanism (Walker-Barnes & Mason, 2001).

Youth are clearly affected by family members' responses to their behavior, whether youth are living at home or in a treatment program. That is why families should be involved in treatment planning and supporting new skills youth learn through treatment. For example, parents of all youth who are involved in Boys Town residential treatment programs are required to complete parenting courses. When implementing social skill instruction, it is crucial that the family is informed about skills the youth is learning and how best to support the youth so he or she can better learn and master those skills.

Peers also exert a large influence on the behavior of youth. Consider the relationship between peer groups and school performance. When a youth's peers do not

25

value academic and behavioral achievement, they will have a negative effect on how the youth behaves and performs at school. For example, consider a youth who is diagnosed with Attention-Deficit/Hyperactivity Disorder (ADHD). The youth may clearly need to learn the skill of "Doing Good Quality Work." However, further assessment might indicate that the youth does not take his time to complete schoolwork because of peer pressure; his peers either hurriedly complete their work or refuse to do it. They also tease youth who take their work seriously. This information can guide the treatment provider to teach target skills like "Resisting Peer Pressure" and "Responding to Teasing," in addition to "Doing Good Quality Work."

Social factors encompass a myriad of variables, including family, peers, and community. All of these variables play a significant role in youth development and behavior. They affect the skills youth deem as important and skills youth have learned. Social context provides an overall understanding of where youth are coming from, which helps guide how treatment should proceed.

Genetic and Biological Considerations

Most psychologists today generally agree that genetics and biology play just as important a role in human behavior as environment. Many mental health disorder diagnoses have been linked to genetic causes. Particular cases of mental retardation like Down's Syndrome and Fragile X are due to genetic syndromes. The biology of individuals with particular disorders such as Attention-Deficit/Hyperactivity Disorder (ADHD) and Anorexia Nervosa (Mash & Barkley, 2007) also has been found to be different. This highlights the importance genetic and biological factors play in the expression and progression of symptoms, and social skills deficits are no exception.

Given the influence that genetic and biological factors have on social skill deficits, it is crucial to include medical professionals as members of any treatment team. Medical professionals like pediatricians and psychiatrists can offer specialized information regarding biologically based aspects of treatment planning. For example, medication is a common treatment plan component when addressing ADHD. When medication is part of a treatment plan, it is essential to involve a doctor who can monitor medication side effects and effectiveness. Another example would be youth who are diagnosed with eating disorders; these disorders can be life-threatening if they are not addressed medically. In fact, hospitalization, medication, and/or nutritional counseling may be necessary. Even when medical treatment plays a primary role in an individualized treatment plan, social skills instruction can play a supportive role by improving diagnosis-related social skill deficits. In these cases, the social skill of "Seeking Professional Assistance" could be a necessary part of the plan.

When working with youth with DSM-IV-TR diagnoses, it is essential that treatment providers help youth understand the role their biology and genetics play in the symptoms they are experiencing. Youth should be made aware that they are not limited by their biology and should learn how to cope with it effectively. Often, this process involves learning social skills, which is what makes skills such a valuable treatment component. (We caution providers to avoid the pitfall of allowing youth to believe they are helpless in the control of their symptoms. Even with disorders that are largely treated by medication, youth still have the responsibility of taking their medication, which is very much within their control.)

Biological factors provide a framework for performance. Even biological elements like metabolic rates, digestion, and sleep can cause and interact with symptoms associated with many DSM-IV-TR diagnoses. Treatment providers also should remember to consider how general medical conditions can influence mental health, as some physical conditions can mimic or exacerbate mental problems. For example, several symptoms associated with hypothyroidism (sluggishness, tiredness, slow speech, negative affect, and reduced appetite) resemble symptoms that also are associated with depression. If possible physical causes are not ruled out through consulting with a youth's physician, hypothyroidism symptoms could be mistaken for symptoms of depression. In some cases, medical tests might be needed before a mental health diagnosis can be made. For example, youth who have encopresis should undergo medical tests to determine if constipation is the cause of soiling. If these youth are found to have constipation, the condition may require more medical intervention than if constipation was absent.

Genetic and biological factors are continuously operating within us. These factors affect us at varying levels and interact with the environment to produce a unique whole that forms mental health. This is why an entire DSM-IV-TR Axis is devoted to general medical conditions. The astute treatment provider is wise to include both individual genetic and biological histories and current biological functioning when making treatment planning decisions. In addition, providers should be ready and willing to include medical professionals in treatment planning discussions in order to develop fully informed plans.

Summary

When developing individualized treatment plans, it's essential to take into account the many factors that influence and shape youth and their behavior. There are developmental, cultural, behavioral, emotional, social, genetic, and biological factors that are unique to each and every youth. Some of these factors will play more prominent roles than others in a youth's treatment. But, all these factors need to be carefully considered from the beginning in order to create an effective treatment plan that has the best opportunity to succeed.

Chapter 3

Social Skills and Mental Health Disorders

Boys Town believes that social skill instruction is an integral element in the successful treatment of youth with mental health and/or behavioral disorders. This belief is based on extensive experience, successful treatment outcomes, and comprehensive research that shows that children and adolescents who struggle with emotional, behavioral, and social problems do get better when they learn prosocial skills.

This chapter will provide an overview of the effectiveness of social skill instruction in the Boys Town Teaching Model, specific outcomes of this skill-based treatment approach in Boys Town's programs, and reasons why teaching skills to troubled youth helps them find success across a variety of settings. We also will discuss how DSM-IV-TR diagnoses can help determine which social skills to target for teaching and what goals to set for treatment.

Social Skill Deficits Versus Performance Deficits

Before we discuss the effective outcomes of social skill teaching, it is important to understand why youth need to learn skills as part of their treatment. Young people require intervention and treatment for many reasons. According to Boys Town's philosophy, the development of behavioral and mental health problems in youth can often be linked to youth not learning the social skills needed to overcome problems. In other words, these youth have a "skill deficit" because they haven't been taught a group of skills or have received inadequate or improper skill instruction. Another possible explanation for why youngsters don't display positive behaviors could be a "performance deficit," which means a youth has been taught a skill and has mastered it but doesn't use it.

Here are two examples of youth with skill deficits:

Kim is a teenager whose mother, Tonya, is the sole caregiver for Kim and her three siblings. Tonya works two jobs to support and provide for her children. She is rarely home, so she usually doesn't have time to prepare home-cooked meals or to eat with her children. Kim, the oldest child, is in charge of feeding her younger siblings. Most days, they eat junk food like potato chips and candy for meals and snack throughout the night. Kim might occasionally heat up frozen foods or canned goods, which the children eat with their hands in front of the television. Kim is often overwhelmed by the premature responsibility of caring for her siblings. Sometimes, at night, she sneaks bags of potato chips or a pint or two of ice cream out of the kitchen to eat as a way to relax and find a sense of contentment. Since Kim hasn't been taught healthy eating habits or skills related to controlling her eating, and has had no opportunity to learn and develop these skills, she has a skill deficit in the area of "Controlling Eating Habits."

Tim, a six-year-old boy, always demands candy while waiting in the checkout line with his mother at the grocery store. Usually, Tim's mother tells him "No." When Tim hears this answer, he immediately begins to scream and cry, creating quite a scene. Even though Tim's mother has talked to him about his negative response, he never accepts "No" for an answer. Tim's mother often gives in and buys him the candy he wants because she's embarrassed and simply wants Tim to calm down and be quiet. In this situation, Tim has failed to acquire the social skill of "Accepting 'No' for an Answer" because his mother has not properly taught it to him.

As for performance deficits, a multitude of reasons could factor into why a youth doesn't display a skill he or she has learned. Some reasons proposed by Bellini (2006) include lack of motivation, sensory sensitivities, anxiety, attention problems, impulsivity, memory problems, self-efficacy deficits, and movement or motor issues.

Let's look at an example of a performance deficit that results from lack of motivation. In this situation, the youth is not internally motivated to use a skill so an external reward the youth values must be implemented.

Josh is a competent student who usually does well on tests. Currently, however, he is failing several classes because he is not completing his homework. Grades aren't a big deal to Josh. He isn't internally motivated to earn A's, and he doesn't see any payoff for getting them. Josh is fully capable of completing his homework; he sometimes does it when it's raining outside just so he has something to do. In this situation, Josh can perform the skill of "Completing Homework" but chooses not to. One way to address this is to set up a contingency where Josh can't go outside to play with his friends until he completes his homework. Most likely, Josh will begin to use the skill because he now has an external motivation (going outside to play) to perform the skill correctly.

The best way treatment providers can differentiate between a skill deficit and a performance deficit is to ask five questions identified by Bellini (2006, p. 115) during the assessment of a youth.

"1. Does the child perform the skill across multiple settings and persons?

2. Does the child perform the skill without support or assistance?

3. Does the child perform the skill fluently and effortlessly?

4. Does the child perform the skill when reinforcement is provided?

5. Does the child perform the skill when environmental modifications are made?"

If the answer to most of these questions is "Yes" during an assessment, it is likely the youth has a performance deficit rather than a skill deficit. If the answer to most of the questions is "No," the youth probably has a skill deficit.

Finally, skill deficits and performance deficits are not always exclusive. It is possible for a youth to not fully acquire a skill *and* not have the motivation to develop and use it. In these cases, both skill training and an intervention that addresses performance (e.g., motivation systems, self-monitoring intervention) are necessary to target combined deficit issues. (The Boys Town Teaching Model addresses both deficit forms by combining social skill training with a token economy.)

Social Skill Instruction and the Boys Town Teaching Model

The overall goal of the Boys Town Teaching Model is to help youth learn how to become productive adults who can make good decisions, interact positively with others in society, and find success in their lives. Two of the Model's hallmarks are teaching social skills and learning how to build positive relationships, both of which result in intrinsic changes within youth. Social skills taught through the Model are very important for youngsters because they provide the foundation upon which many other more complex and advanced skills can be built. Acquiring these "keystone" self-help skills opens up a myriad of possibilities for change – emotionally, behaviorally, and socially – that otherwise might not have been present.

By learning self-help skills, children can change the way they think, feel, and act. This is a learning process. Boys Town's teaching methods utilize behavioral principles while allowing children to integrate their thoughts and feelings into this learning process. Boys Town also uses external reinforcement, where appropriate, to promote and maintain skill-learning and relationship development. As changes in external behavior occur, internal shifts also occur. These enable youth to change intrinsically. Inadequate thought patterns are reframed, negative feelings diminish, and inappropriate behaviors are replaced by positive behaviors, which benefit both the youth and those who interact with them.

As we stress the importance and benefits of social skill instruction for youth with mental health disorders, it is imperative for treatment providers to understand that the success youth achieve in Boys Town programs results not only from learning social skills but from a complete and comprehensive treatment environment. Youth in Boys Town programs – especially those in long-term residential settings – live and learn in a highly structured environment where therapeutic treatment is a part of everything they do. The positive outcomes of youth treatment involving social skill instruction that will be presented later in this chapter must be understood in the context of a larger treatment approach. (For a more detailed description of the role social skill instruction plays in the Boys Town Teaching Model, see *Teaching Social Skills to Youth, A Step-by-Step Guide to 182 Basic to Complex Skills Plus Helpful Teaching Techniques, Second Edition*, by Tom Dowd and Jeff Tierney, published by the Boys Town Press.)

Fundamentals of Skill-Based Treatment

The environments of troubled youth who require treatment significantly contribute to and foster the formation of their problem behaviors and mental health difficulties. However, these learned inappropriate behaviors and skills serve a purpose. They enable youth to get what they need and want and/or avoid something they don't like or don't want. Over time, these same behaviors and skills become reinforced and strengthened, and eventually spill over in to other environments (school, extracurricular activities, jobs, relationships with peers and adults, and so on).

When youth with strong learning histories that support negative behavior encounter new environments or settings, they typically use the same negative behaviors that were successful for them in the past. When these behaviors don't work, kids flounder, unsure of what it takes to be successful. For youth to succeed in familiar and unfamiliar environments, situations, and relationships, they must learn new prosocial skills that will help them get their needs and wants met in ways that are more socially acceptable. This is the aim of the Boys Town Teaching Model and the role of social skill instruction.

Boys Town's social skill instruction approach to treatment focuses on teaching the essential life skills young people need in order to make the successful transition into young adulthood (Peter, 1999). Social, academic, and vocational skills, as well as spiritual values, are taught in a "family-style" treatment setting through proactively teaching at neutral times, reinforcing positive behavior as it occurs, practicing and rehearsing, correcting inappropriate behavior in a positive style, and helping youth learn to use alternative appropriate behaviors when they face crisis situations.

According to Gresham (1998, p.20), a social skill is defined as "...socially acceptable learned behaviors enabling the individual to interact effectively with others and avoid or escape socially unacceptable behavior exhibited by others." Thus, social skills enable youth to appropriately and effectively behave in the various environments they inhabit (home, school, work, etc.). These skills not only produce positive consequences for the individual but also are socially acceptable and responsive to others.

With social skill instruction, youth learn skills that are determined to be the most functional for them and expected to produce the best long-term results. This means that every youth requires individual treatment. As discussed in Chapter 2, some youth will initially need to learn the most basic skills ("Following Instructions," "Accepting Consequences," "Accepting 'No' for an Answer," etc.) in order to lay a foundation for more complex skills ("Expressing Feelings Appropriately," "Resisting Peer Pressure," "Using Spontaneous Problem-Solving," etc.). Many times, treatment providers will need to gradually shape a youth's behavior by patiently teaching basic social skills so that the youth can learn the final desired behavior. This can be a slow, arduous process for treatment providers and youth, but it is necessary if the youth is to overcome his or her problems. (Eight basic social skills and their steps are provided in the Appendix.)

The use of appropriate social skills involves an immensely complex chain of rapidly occurring interpersonal events. For youth, especially those suffering from mental health disorders that dramatically limit their emotional and behavioral functioning, correctly performing these skills at the right time can be an overwhelming task. They may have considerable difficulty organizing and blending their behaviors into smooth-flowing interactions with others, particularly under stressful conditions. So, treatment providers must be able and willing to adjust their teaching techniques, vocabulary, and interpersonal behaviors to best meet the learning style of each youth in their care.

When choosing social skills for treatment, it is important for providers to take into account individual factors like the age and developmental level of the youth, severity of the youth's behaviors, the length of time a youth has been exposed to social skill instruction, and other factors discussed in Chapter 2. Individual considerations play a pivotal role in the success or failure of each youth's treatment plan. Once the most appropriate skills have been identified and prioritized, treatment providers can utilize the various teaching interactions developed at Boys Town to reinforce and teach youth new, prosocial ways of getting their needs met.

Boys Town's Social Skill Curriculum contains 182 skills that address a wide variety of youth issues at all levels, from minor school- or home-related problems to skill deficits associated with more serious problems like aggression, delinquency, and depression. All 182 curriculum skills, the steps to each skill, and the teaching interactions that form the cornerstone of treatment planning and active intervention at Boys Town are presented in Boys Town's book, *Teaching Social Skills to Youth, A Step-by-step Guide to 182 Basic to Complex Skills Plus Helpful Teaching Techniques, Second Edition.* The Social Skill Curriculum and teaching techniques described in that book can be easily integrated into a variety of settings (natural home environment, foster home, emergency shelter care program, group home residential program, psychiatric treatment program, and many others).

A Proven, Effective Treatment Strategy

How do we know that social skill instruction – one of the hallmarks of the Boys Town Teaching Model – is a therapeutic, effective treatment strategy? For starters, the Boys Town Teaching Model grew out of behavioral research conducted by Montrose Wolf, one of the pioneers in the applied behavior analysis movement. In the late 1960s and early 1970s, Wolf and his colleagues began their research to design a new treatment model for troubled youth as an effective alternative to the standard state-run programs of the time. The new model came to be known as the Teaching-Family Model, and it was adopted by Boys Town in 1975 (Risley, 2005). The Teaching-Family Model has been tested time and time again, across numerous settings and behavior problems, with positive results (Fixsen, Blasé, Timbers, & Wolf, 2001).

The Teaching-Family Model combines multiple components including a token-economy motivation system, detailed specification and monitoring of the desired behaviors, and skill teaching of desired behaviors. All this takes place within a family home setting where the primary "teachers" or "house parents" are a married couple (Wolf, Kirigin, Fixen, Blasé, & Braukmann, 1995). The Boys Town Teaching Model, which is used in all Boys Town programs, utilizes the components previously listed, with a specific focus on teaching social skills.

While youth are treated at Boys Town, a variety of data is gathered. Standardized outcome instruments like those discussed in Chapter 1 (CBCL, DISC, etc.) are frequently administered to youth. Improvements on these instruments often occur because youth learn and successfully use the social skills that are taught as part of their treatment. For example, an examination of the admission and departure Child Behavior Checklist (CBCL) scores for youth who left the Boys Town Treatment Family Home Program between 2001 and 2004 revealed that eighty percent of the girls and sixty-three percent of the boys were admitted with a CBCL total score in the clinically significant range. Remarkably, these scores had dropped to twenty-five percent for girls and twenty-four percent for boys by the time these youth departed the program (Figure 1).

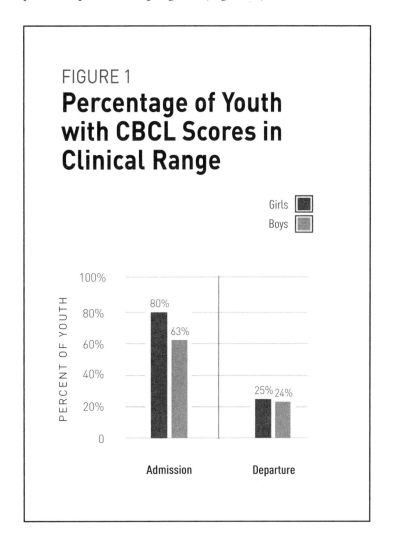

FIGURE 1

Percentage of Youth with CBCL Scores in Clinical Range

Further, youth admitted during this same time frame arrived with a variety of mental health issues that improved significantly during treatment. For example, seventy-two percent of girls and fifty-four percent of boys were admitted with a DSM-IV-TR diagnosis. Twelve months later, only thirty percent of girls and twenty-four percent of boys continued to meet criteria for a formal DSM-IV-TR diagnosis (Figure 2) (Boys Town National Research Institute for Child and Family Studies, 2006a).

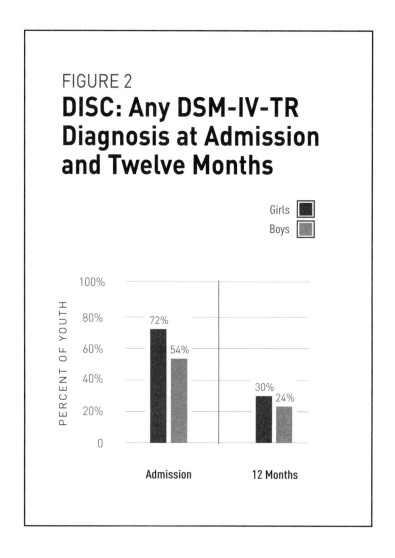

FIGURE 2

DISC: Any DSM-IV-TR Diagnosis at Admission and Twelve Months

Longitudinal outcome research suggests that the effects of treatment at Boys Town continue after youth depart from the program. One such study, an extensive sixteen-year follow-up completed in 2003, involved 211 former Boys Town youth and forty-one "comparison" youth who were accepted for admission to Boys Town but never came. Participants, ages twenty-seven to thirty-seven, completed a 151-item survey measuring several life domains. Results produced two major findings: 1) As adults, those participants who received treatment at Boys Town were more likely to be functioning as productive, law-abiding citizens than those who did not, and 2) the longer these former Boys Town youth were in the treatment program, the more positive the long-term outcomes. For example, when looking at criminality, the youth who received eighteen months or more of treatment at Boys Town had lower rates of incarceration, recent arrests, criminal activity, and Intimate Partner Violence (IPV) than those youth who received six months of treatment or less (Figure 3) (Huefner, Ringle, Chmelka, & Ingram, 2007; Ringle, Chmelka, Ingram, & Huefner, 2006).

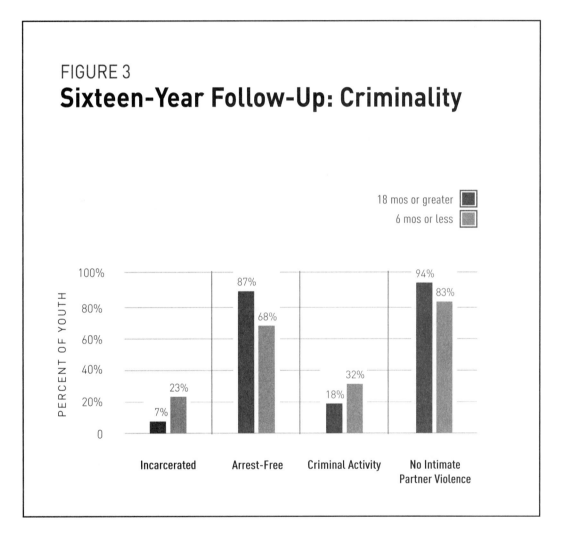

FIGURE 3
Sixteen-Year Follow-Up: Criminality

In 2006, the Boys Town National Research Institute completed a five-year follow-up study of Boys Town youth who departed in the year 2000. Approximately two hundred former Boys Town youth (with an average age of twenty-one) responded to an eighty-five-item survey that measured social functioning and quality of life across a variety of domains. These youth entered care with a variety of risk factors, including school problems, being out-of-parental control, aggression, depression, substance use, and interpersonal problems. Five years after leaving treatment, the former Boys Town youth were functioning similar to their peers in the general population in areas like education, employment, and overall positive mental health (Figure 4). These outcomes provide strong evidence of the efficacy of the Boys Town Teaching Model in teaching lasting social skills to youth who are struggling within everyday society (Thompson, Ringle, & Kingsley, 2007).

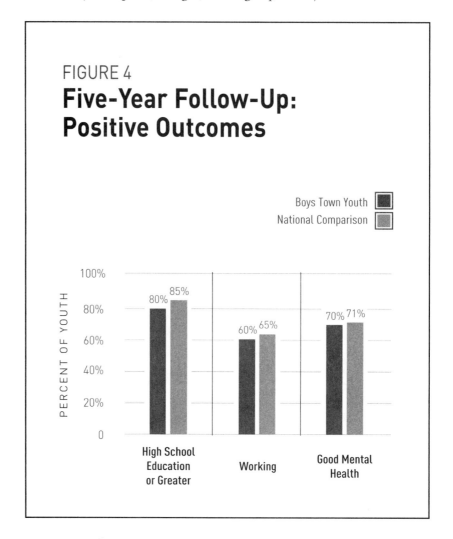

FIGURE 4

Five-Year Follow-Up: Positive Outcomes

We believe all the research presented here, as well as numerous other positive findings (e.g., Handwerk et al., 2008; Larzelere, Daly, Davis, Chmelka, & Handwerk, 2004; Thompson et al., 1996), verify that the Boys Town Teaching Model, with its emphasis on social skill training, is an effective, therapeutic treatment option. Just as other strategies (psychotropic medication; individual, family, or group therapy; and behavioral interventions) are prescribed as part of a youth's treatment plan, so too are the specific social skills that youth need to learn. Once youth have mastered these skills, they are better able to appropriately and effectively interact with their environment and those in it.

Summary

The core of the Boys Town Teaching Model involves teaching youth social skills and how to build relationships. The Model incorporates a social skill instruction approach – teaching youth positive alternative skills that can replace negative behaviors – while also recognizing the importance and need for other types of treatment strategies like medications and therapy, as important ingredients to an overall treatment plan. Equally important to successful treatment planning are prescribing and assigning suitable social skills for targeted teaching by treatment providers. Boys Town's extensive research has shown that social skill instruction, in a wide variety of treatment settings, is a valuable and effective treatment option for helping troubled youth overcome their problems.

Chapter 4

Social Skill Charts for Specific Mental Health Disorders

The charts presented in this chapter are helpful guides for including social skill instruction in individualized treatment plans for youth with mental health disorders. Treatment teams that use these charts can more easily and efficiently identify and prescribe social skills that are appropriate for a specific DSM-IV-TR diagnosis and individually suited to meet each child's treatment goals.

The charts are arranged by the order and sections used in the DSM-IV-TR. The diagnoses and social skills covered in the charts were selected by a panel of youth-care experts at Boys Town. Not all diagnoses or sections from the DSM-IV-TR are listed because some diagnoses do not readily lend themselves to social skill instruction or are not commonly diagnosed in children and adolescents.

For each DSM-IV-TR diagnosis, there is a list of suggested social skills. In some cases, the skills are combined for several disorders within a section that may be associated with similar skill deficits. Suggested social skills are ones treatment providers can target and teach to youth who have a particular disorder and are lacking in certain skill areas. The skills are grouped according to their level of mastery – basic, intermediate, advanced, and complex.

Treatment providers can use the skill lists during the treatment planning process to help determine appropriate goals and objectives for youth with particular mental health disorders. Selections of specific skills should not be based solely on a DSM-IV-TR diagnosis, but rather on specific referral concerns and current problems youth are exhibiting. It is important to remember that treatment planning – including determining which social skills to teach – should be individualized to meet the specific needs of each child. Even when youth are diagnosed with the same disorder, skill deficits or performance deficits will vary, and each youth will display symptoms associated with a diagnosis differently. Usually, a treatment team will choose skills that address a youth's specific deficits and needs and help meet his or her overall treatment goals. For example, after evaluating two youth who are diagnosed with Posttraumatic Stress Disorder, the treatment team might recommend teaching the social skill of "Saying 'No' Assertively" for one youth because she relaxed her personal boundaries following her trauma experience. The team then might recommend teaching the social skill of "Participating in Activities" for the second youth because he has been withdrawn since his trauma experience. Ultimately, a youth's individual expression of his or her diagnosis and particular social skills deficits, as well as individual considerations (developmental, cultural, social, etc.), should guide decisions on what specific skills to target for treatment.

As the treatment planning process for social skills training begins and unfolds, treatment providers can use the appropriate charts to select skills that best fit a youngster's treatment needs. Let's look at an example of how this might work. Carla is a sixteen-year-old who has been diagnosed with Reactive Attachment Disorder. She has been admitted to a residential group home facility because she frequently yells and curses at her adopted parents, doesn't follow instructions at home and school, hangs out with inappropriate friends, and engages in promiscuous activity with multiple male peers.

At the first treatment team meeting, the team determines that the primary goal for Carla will be to build positive relationships with others. Next, the team looks at the social skills listed on the charts for Reactive Attachment Disorder to identify skills to teach Carla that would help her meet this goal and skill deficit objective. After identifying skills and objectives, the team determines how progress is to be monitored for each objective and what level of improvement they expect for each objective before the next team meeting. Throughout the meeting, team members consider Carla's individual characteristics to ensure that the social skills and other components of the treatment plan meet her individual needs.

Since Carla's primary difficulty is with male peers, one skill selected for the goal of building positive relationships is "Setting Appropriate Boundaries." School staff will monitor Carla's progress with this skill since school is the primary setting where Carla interacts with male peers. School staff will record positive and negative interactions with males on a behavior card as they occur. Since Carla has shown she is not able to use the skill of "Setting Appropriate Boundaries," the initial goal is modest; however, expectations will increase as Carla practices the skill and shows progress. The team decides that a three-to-one ratio of positive-to-negative interactions with males is a realistic starting goal. The team uses this same process to select other skills and objectives that fit the goal of building positive relationships with others, and members identify two more goals and social skills from the Reactive Attachment Disorder chart for those goals, based on Carla's current symptoms and history. After the team meeting, Carla's youth care supervisor writes out an individualized treatment plan, which includes the appropriate social skills to be taught, based on the results and conclusions of the treatment team meeting.

A good treatment plan is the first step to effective treatment. When treatment providers use the kind of treatment planning process just outlined, along with the charts that follow, they can better select the social skills that best fit each youth's treatment plans and individual needs.

Disorders Usually Diagnosed in Infancy, Childhood, or Adolescence

MENTAL RETARDATION

Suggested Social Skills Training for Individuals Diagnosed with Mild Mental Retardation

BASIC SKILLS

- Accepting Criticism or a Consequence
- Accepting "No" for an Answer
- Disagreeing Appropriately
- Following Instructions
- Introducing Yourself
- Talking with Others

INTERMEDIATE SKILLS

- Accepting Apologies from Others
- Accepting Compliments
- Accepting Consequences
- Accepting Decisions of Authority
- Answering the Telephone
- Asking for Help
- Asking Questions
- Checking In (or Checking Back)
- Closing a Conversation
- Completing Tasks
- Complying with Reasonable Requests
- Contributing to Discussions (Joining in a Conversation)
- Doing Good Quality Work
- Following Rules
- Getting Another Person's Attention
- Getting the Teacher's Attention

- Giving Compliments
- Greeting Others
- Ignoring Distractions by Others
- Initiating a Conversation
- Interrupting Appropriately
- Introducing Others
- Listening to Others
- Maintaining a Conversation
- Maintaining an Appropriate Appearance
- Making an Apology
- Making a Request (Asking a Favor)
- Making a Telephone Call
- Participating in Activities
- Reporting Emergencies
- Reporting Other Youths' Behavior (or Peer Reporting)
- Resisting Peer Pressure
- Saying Good-Bye to Guests
- Saying "No" Assertively
- Seeking Positive Attention
- Showing Appreciation
- Staying on Task
- Trying New Tasks
- Using an Appropriate Voice Tone

Mental Retardation (Cont)

- Using Anger Control Strategies
- Using Table Etiquette
- Waiting Your Turn

ADVANCED SKILLS

- Accepting Defeat or Loss
- Accepting Help or Assistance
- Accepting Winning Appropriately
- Caring for Others' Property
- Caring for Own Belongings
- Choosing Appropriate Clothing
- Choosing Appropriate Friends
- Communicating Honestly
- Concentrating on a Subject or Task
- Contributing to Group Activities
- Controlling Eating Habits
- Coping with Anger and Aggression from Others
- Coping with Change
- Coping with Conflict
- Coping with Sad Feelings (or Depression)
- Dealing with Being Left Out
- Dealing with Boredom
- Dealing with Contradictory Messages
- Dealing with Failure
- Dealing with Fear
- Dealing with Frustration
- Dealing with Group Pressure
- Dealing with Rejection
- Delaying Gratification

- Displaying Effort
- Displaying Sportsmanship
- Expressing Appropriate Affection
- Expressing Feelings Appropriately
- Expressing Pride in Accomplishments
- Following Safety Rules
- Interacting Appropriately with the Opposite Sex
- Keeping Property in Its Place
- Lending to Others
- Making New Friends
- Organizing Tasks and Activities
- Persevering on Tasks and Projects
- Planning Meals
- Preparing for a Stressful Conversation
- Preventing Trouble with Others
- Responding to Others' Humor
- Responding to Teasing
- Self-Reporting Own Behaviors
- Setting Appropriate Boundaries
- Sharing Attention with Others
- Sharing Personal Experiences
- Suggesting an Activity
- Using Appropriate Humor
- Using Appropriate Language
- Using Relaxation Strategies
- Using Self-Talk or Self-Instruction

Mental Retardation (Cont)

COMPLEX SKILLS

- Asking for Advice
- Assessing Own Abilities
- Being a Consumer
- Being Assertive
- Being Patient
- Budgeting and Managing Money
- Differentiating Friends from Acquaintances
- Displaying Appropriate Control
- Identifying Own Feelings
- Interviewing for a Job
- Maintaining Relationships
- Making an Appropriate Complaint
- Recognizing Moods of Others
- Resolving Conflicts
- Seeking Professional Assistance
- Using Community Resources
- Using Leisure Time
- Using Strategies to Find a Job

LEARNING DISORDERS

Reading Disorder
Mathematics
Disorder of Written Expression
Learning Disorder, Not Otherwise Specified (NOS)

Suggested Social Skills Training for Individuals Diagnosed with a Learning Disorder

BASIC SKILLS

- Accepting Criticism or a Consequence
- Following Instructions

INTERMEDIATE SKILLS

- Asking for Clarification
- Asking for Help
- Asking Questions
- Checking In (or Checking Back)
- Choosing Appropriate Words to Say
- Completing Homework
- Completing Tasks
- Doing Good Quality Work
- Following Written Instructions
- Getting the Teacher's Attention
- Ignoring Distractions by Others
- Listening to Others
- Making Positive Self-Statements
- Participating in Activities
- Staying on Task

ADVANCED SKILLS

- Accepting Help or Assistance
- Advocating for Oneself
- Analyzing Skills Needed for Different Situations
- Analyzing Tasks to be Completed
- Being Prepared for Class
- Concentrating on a Subject or Task
- Contributing to Group Activities
- Controlling Emotions
- Dealing with Failure
- Dealing with Frustration
- Displaying Effort
- Expressing Feelings Appropriately
- Expressing Optimism
- Expressing Pride in Accomplishments
- Organizing Tasks and Activities
- Persevering on Tasks and Projects
- Responding to Teasing
- Responding to Written Requests
- Self-Correcting Own Behavior
- Using Relaxation Strategies
- Using Self-Talk or Self-Instruction
- Using Study Skills
- Working Independently

Learning Disorders (Cont)

COMPLEX SKILLS

- Accepting Self
- Asking for Advice
- Assessing Own Abilities
- Being Patient
- Budgeting and Managing Money
- Formulating Strategies
- Gathering Information
- Interviewing for a Job
- Managing Stress
- Rewarding Yourself
- Setting Goals
- Using Community Resources
- Using Self-Monitoring and Self-Reflection
- Using Strategies to Find a Job

PERVASIVE DEVELOPMENTAL DISORDERS

Asperger's Disorder
Pervasive Developmental Disorder,
Not Otherwise Specified

Suggested Social Skills Training for Individuals Diagnosed with Asperger's Disorder or Pervasive Developmental Disorder, NOS

BASIC SKILLS

- Accepting Criticism or a Consequence
- Accepting "No" for an Answer
- Disagreeing Appropriately
- Following Instructions
- Introducing Yourself
- Showing Respect
- Showing Sensitivity to Others
- Talking with Others

INTERMEDIATE SKILLS

- Accepting Apologies from Others
- Accepting Compliments
- Accepting Consequences
- Accepting Decisions of Authority
- Answering the Telephone
- Asking for Clarification
- Asking for Help
- Asking Questions
- Checking In (or Checking Back)
- Choosing Appropriate Words to Say
- Closing a Conversation
- Complying with Reasonable Requests
- Contributing to Discussions (Joining in a Conversation)
- Correcting Another Person (or Giving Criticism)

- Getting Another Person's Attention
- Getting the Teacher's Attention
- Giving Compliments
- Greeting Others
- Ignoring Distractions by Others
- Initiating a Conversation
- Interrupting Appropriately
- Introducing Others
- Listening to Others
- Maintaining a Conversation
- Maintaining an Appropriate Appearance
- Making a Request (Asking a Favor)
- Making a Telephone Call
- Making Positive Self-Statements
- Making Positive Statements about Others
- Offering Assistance or Help
- Participating in Activities
- Reporting Other Youths' Behavior (or Peer Reporting)
- Resisting Peer Pressure
- Saying Good-Bye to Guests
- Saying "No" Assertively
- Seeking Positive Attention
- Showing Appreciation
- Showing Interest

Pervasive Developmental Disorders (Cont)

- Trying New Tasks
- Using an Appropriate Voice Tone
- Using Anger Control Strategies
- Using Structured Problem Solving (SODAS)
- Using Table Etiquette
- Volunteering
- Waiting Your Turn

ADVANCED SKILLS

- Accepting Defeat or Loss
- Accepting Help or Assistance
- Accepting Winning Appropriately
- Advocating for Oneself
- Analyzing Skills Needed for Different Situations
- Analyzing Social Situations
- Compromising with Others
- Contributing to Group Activities
- Controlling Emotions
- Cooperating with Others
- Coping with Anger and Aggression from Others
- Coping with Change
- Coping with Conflict
- Coping with Sad Feelings (or Depression)
- Dealing with Accusations
- Dealing with Being Left Out
- Dealing with Boredom
- Dealing with Contradictory Messages
- Dealing with Embarrassing Situations
- Dealing with Failure
- Dealing with Fear

- Dealing with Frustration
- Dealing with Group Pressure
- Dealing with Rejection
- Delaying Gratification
- Displaying Effort
- Displaying Sportsmanship
- Expressing Appropriate Affection
- Expressing Feelings Appropriately
- Expressing Optimism
- Expressing Pride in Accomplishments
- Following Through on Agreements and Contracts
- Giving Instructions
- Giving Rationales
- Interacting Appropriately with the Opposite Sex
- Lending to Others
- Making New Friends
- Making Restitution (Compensating)
- Negotiating with Others
- Preparing for a Stressful Conversation
- Preventing Trouble with Others
- Problem-Solving a Disagreement
- Responding to Complaints
- Responding to Others' Feelings
- Responding to Others' Humor
- Responding to Teasing
- Self-Correcting Own Behavior
- Self-Reporting Own Behaviors
- Setting Appropriate Boundaries
- Sharing Attention with Others
- Sharing Personal Experiences
- Suggesting an Activity
- Using Appropriate Humor

Pervasive Developmental Disorders (Cont)

- Using Relaxation Strategies
- Using Self-Talk or Self-Instruction
- Using Spontaneous Problem-Solving

COMPLEX SKILLS

- Accepting Self
- Altering One's Environment
- Asking for Advice
- Assessing Own Abilities
- Being Assertive
- Being Patient
- Differentiating Friends from Acquaintances
- Displaying Appropriate Control
- Expressing Empathy and Understanding for Others
- Expressing Grief
- Identifying Own Feelings
- Laughing at Oneself
- Maintaining Relationships
- Making an Appropriate Complaint
- Managing Stress
- Recognizing Moods of Others
- Resolving Conflicts
- Taking Risks Appropriately
- Using Self-Monitoring and Self-Reflection

ATTENTION DEFICIT AND DISRUPTIVE DISORDERS

Attention-Deficit/Hyperactivity Disorder
Attention-Deficit/Hyperactivity Disorder, Not Otherwise Specified

Suggested Social Skills Training for Individuals Diagnosed with an Attention-Deficit/ Hyperactivity Disorder

BASIC SKILLS

- Accepting Criticism or a Consequence
- Accepting "No" for an Answer
- Disagreeing Appropriately
- Following Instructions
- Showing Respect

INTERMEDIATE SKILLS

- Accepting Compliments
- Accepting Consequences
- Accepting Decisions of Authority
- Being on Time (Promptness)
- Checking In (or Checking Back)
- Choosing Appropriate Words to Say
- Completing Homework
- Completing Tasks
- Complying with Reasonable Requests
- Doing Good Quality Work
- Following Written Instructions
- Getting Another Person's Attention
- Getting the Teacher's Attention
- Ignoring Distractions by Others
- Interrupting Appropriately
- Listening to Others
- Resisting Peer Pressure

- Saying "No" Assertively
- Seeking Positive Attention
- Staying on Task
- Using an Appropriate Voice Tone
- Using Anger Control Strategies
- Using Structured Problem-Solving (SODAS)
- Waiting Your Turn

ADVANCED SKILLS

- Accepting Defeat or Loss
- Accepting Winning Appropriately
- Analyzing Skills Needed for Different Situations
- Analyzing Social Situations
- Analyzing Tasks to Be Completed
- Being Prepared for Class
- Concentrating on a Subject or Task
- Controlling Emotions
- Coping with Anger and Aggression from Others
- Coping with Conflict
- Dealing with Being Left Out
- Dealing with Boredom
- Dealing with Failure

Attention Deficit and Disruptive Disorders (Cont)

- Dealing with Frustration
- Dealing with Group Pressure
- Dealing with Rejection
- Delaying Gratification
- Displaying Effort
- Displaying Sportsmanship
- Expressing Feelings Appropriately
- Following Through on Agreements and Contracts
- Making Decisions
- Managing Time
- Organizing Tasks and Activities
- Persevering on Tasks and Projects
- Preventing Trouble with Others
- Problem-Solving a Disagreement
- Responding to Complaints
- Responding to Teasing
- Responding to Written Requests
- Self-Correcting Own Behavior
- Sharing Attention with Others
- Using Appropriate Humor
- Using Spontaneous Problem Solving
- Using Study Skills
- Working Independently

COMPLEX SKILLS

- Altering One's Environment
- Being Assertive
- Being Patient
- Budgeting and Managing Money
- Displaying Appropriate Control
- Formulating Strategies
- Gathering Information
- Planning Ahead
- Resolving Conflicts
- Setting Goals
- Taking Risks Appropriately
- Using Leisure Time
- Using Self-Monitoring and Self-Reflection

CONDUCT DISORDER

Oppositional Defiant Disorder
Disruptive Behavior Disorder, Not Otherwise Specified

Suggested Social Skills Training for Individuals Diagnosed with Conduct Disorder, Oppositional Defiant Disorder, or Disruptive Behavior Disorder, NOS

BASIC SKILLS

- Accepting Criticism or a Consequence
- Accepting "No" for an Answer
- Disagreeing Appropriately
- Following Instructions
- Showing Respect
- Showing Sensitivity to Others
- Talking with Others

INTERMEDIATE SKILLS

- Accepting Consequences
- Accepting Decisions of Authority
- Checking In (or Checking Back)
- Choosing Appropriate Words to Say
- Complying with Reasonable Requests
- Following Rules
- Getting Another Person's Attention
- Giving Compliments
- Greeting Others
- Interrupting Appropriately
- Listening to Others
- Making an Apology
- Making Positive Statements about Others
- Offering Assistance or Help
- Refraining from Possessing Contraband or Drugs
- Reporting Other Youths' Behavior (or Peer Reporting)

- Resisting Peer Pressure
- Saying "No" Assertively
- Showing Appreciation
- Showing Interest
- Using an Appropriate Voice Tone
- Using Anger Control Strategies
- Using Structured Problem-Solving (SODAS)

ADVANCED SKILLS

- Accepting Defeat or Loss
- Accepting Winning Appropriately
- Analyzing Social Situations
- Borrowing from Others
- Caring for Others' Property
- Caring for Own Belongings
- Choosing Appropriate Friends
- Communicating Honestly
- Complying with School Dress Code
- Compromising with Others
- Controlling Emotions
- Controlling Sexually Abusive Impulses toward Others
- Controlling the Impulse to Lie
- Controlling the Impulse to Steal
- Cooperating with Others
- Coping with Anger and Aggression from Others
- Coping with Conflict
- Dealing with an Accusation

Conduct Disorder (Cont)

- Dealing with Boredom
- Dealing with Frustration
- Dealing with Group Pressure
- Dealing with Rejection
- Delaying Gratification
- Displaying Effort
- Expressing Appropriate Affection
- Expressing Feelings Appropriately
- Following Safety Rules
- Following Through on Agreements and Contracts
- Interacting Appropriately with the Opposite Sex
- Keeping Property in Its Place
- Making Decisions
- Making New Friends
- Making Restitution (Compensating)
- Negotiating with Others
- Preventing Trouble with Others
- Problem-Solving a Disagreement
- Responding to Complaints
- Responding to Others' Feelings
- Responding to Others' Humor
- Responding to Teasing
- Self-Correcting Own Behavior
- Self-Reporting Own Behaviors
- Setting Appropriate Boundaries
- Sharing Attention with Others
- Sharing Personal Experiences
- Using Appropriate Humor
- Using Appropriate Language
- Using Self-Talk or Self-Instruction
- Using Spontaneous Problem-Solving

COMPLEX SKILLS

- Being an Appropriate Role Model
- Being Assertive
- Being Patient
- Clarifying Values and Beliefs
- Differentiating Friends from Acquaintances
- Displaying Appropriate Control
- Expressing Empathy and Understanding for Others
- Formulating Strategies
- Identifying Own Feelings
- Maintaining Relationships
- Making Moral and Spiritual Decisions
- Resolving Conflicts
- Seeking Professional Assistance
- Tolerating Differences
- Using Leisure Time
- Using Self-Monitoring and Self-Reflection

TIC DISORDERS

Tourette's Disorder

Chronic Motor or Vocal TIC Disorder

Transient TIC Disorder

TIC Disorder, Not Otherwise Specified

Suggested Social Skills Training for Individuals Diagnosed with a TIC Disorder

BASIC SKILLS

- Talking with Others

INTERMEDIATE SKILLS

- Making Positive Self-Statements

ADVANCED SKILLS

- Controlling Emotions
- Coping with Conflict
- Dealing with Embarrassing Situations
- Dealing with Frustration
- Dealing with Rejection
- Expressing Feelings Appropriately
- Preparing for a Stressful Conversation
- Responding to Teasing
- Self-Correcting Own Behavior
- Using Relaxation Strategies

COMPLEX SKILLS

- Accepting Self
- Altering One's Environment
- Displaying Appropriate Control
- Managing Stress
- Rewarding Yourself
- Seeking Professional Assistance
- Setting Goals
- Using Self-Monitoring and Self-Reflection

ELIMINATION DISORDERS

Encopresis
Enuresis (Not Due to a General Medical Condition)

Suggested Social Skills Training for Individuals Diagnosed with an Elimination Disorder

BASIC SKILLS

- Accepting Criticism or a Consequence

INTERMEDIATE SKILLS

- Maintaining Personal Hygiene
- Making Positive Self-Statements

ADVANCED SKILLS

- Advocating for Oneself
- Dealing with Embarrassing Situations
- Dealing with Rejection
- Displaying Effort
- Expressing Feelings Appropriately
- Expressing Optimism
- Responding to Teasing
- Self-Reporting Own Behaviors
- Sharing Personal Experiences

COMPLEX SKILLS

- Formulating Strategies
- Rewarding Yourself
- Setting Goals

OTHER DISORDERS OF INFANCY, CHILDHOOD, OR ADOLESCENCE

Separation Anxiety Disorder

Suggested Social Skills Training for Individuals Diagnosed with Separation Anxiety Disorder

BASIC SKILLS

- Talking with Others

INTERMEDIATE SKILLS

- Asking for Help
- Seeking Positive Attention

ADVANCED SKILLS

- Controlling Emotions
- Coping with Change
- Dealing with Fear
- Expressing Feelings Appropriately
- Expressing Optimism
- Self-Correcting Own Behavior
- Using Relaxation Strategies
- Using Self-Talk or Self-Instruction

COMPLEX SKILLS

- Displaying Appropriate Control
- Managing Stress
- Rewarding Yourself
- Setting Goals
- Taking Risks Appropriately
- Using Self-Monitoring and Self-Reflection

Selective Mutism

Suggested Social Skills Training for Individuals Diagnosed with Selective Mutism

BASIC SKILLS

- Talking with Others
- Introducing Yourself

INTERMEDIATE SKILLS

- Accepting Compliments
- Accepting Consequences
- Answering the Telephone
- Asking for Help
- Asking Questions
- Closing a Conversation
- Contributing to Discussions (Joining in a Conversation)
- Getting Another Person's Attention
- Getting the Teacher's Attention
- Greeting Others
- Initiating a Conversation
- Introducing Others
- Maintaining a Conversation
- Participating in Activities
- Saying "No" Assertively
- Showing Appreciation
- Showing Interest

ADVANCED SKILLS

- Analyzing Skills Needed for Different Situations
- Analyzing Social Situations
- Contributing to Group Activities
- Displaying Effort
- Expressing Feelings Appropriately
- Making New Friends
- Preparing for a Stressful Conversation
- Responding to Others' Feelings
- Responding to Others' Humor
- Responding to Teasing
- Using Self-Talk or Self-Instruction

COMPLEX SKILLS

- Being Assertive
- Rewarding Yourself
- Setting Goals
- Taking Risks Appropriately
- Using Self-Monitoring and Self-Reflection

Reactive Attachment Disorder of Infancy or Early Childhood

Suggested Social Skills Training for Individuals Diagnosed with Reactive Attachment Disorder

BASIC SKILLS

- Accepting Criticism or a Consequence
- Introducing Yourself
- Showing Respect
- Showing Sensitivity to Others
- Talking with Others

INTERMEDIATE SKILLS

- Accepting Apologies from Others
- Accepting Compliments
- Accepting Consequences
- Accepting Decisions of Authority
- Asking for Help
- Checking In (or Checking Back)
- Choosing Appropriate Words to Say
- Closing a Conversation
- Complying with Reasonable Requests
- Contributing to Discussions (Joining in a Conversation)
- Correcting Another Person (or Giving Criticism)
- Getting Another Person's Attention
- Getting the Teacher's Attention
- Giving Compliments
- Greeting Others
- Initiating a Conversation
- Interrupting Appropriately
- Introducing Others
- Listening to Others

- Maintaining a Conversation
- Making an Apology
- Making a Request (Asking a Favor)
- Making Positive Self-Statements
- Making Positive Statements about Others
- Offering Assistance or Help
- Participating in Activities
- Saying Good-Bye to Guests
- Saying "No" Assertively
- Seeking Positive Attention
- Showing Appreciation
- Showing Interest
- Using Anger Control Strategies
- Using Structured Problem-Solving (SODAS)
- Volunteering
- Waiting Your Turn

ADVANCED SKILLS

- Accepting Help or Assistance
- Analyzing Skills Needed for Different Situations
- Analyzing Social Situations
- Caring for Others' Property
- Caring for Own Belongings
- Choosing Appropriate Friends
- Communicating Honestly
- Compromising with Others
- Controlling Emotions

Reactive Attachment Disorder of Infancy or Early Childhood (Cont)

- Controlling the Impulse to Lie
- Controlling the Impulse to Steal
- Coping with Change
- Coping with Conflict
- Coping with Sad Feelings (or Depression)
- Dealing with an Accusation
- Dealing with Frustration
- Expressing Appropriate Affection
- Expressing Feelings Appropriately
- Following Through on Agreements and Contracts
- Making New Friends
- Making Restitution (Compensating)
- Negotiating with Others
- Preparing for a Stressful Conversation
- Preventing Trouble with Others
- Problem-Solving a Disagreement
- Responding to Complaints
- Responding to Others' Feelings
- Self-Correcting Own Behavior
- Self-Reporting Own Behaviors
- Setting Appropriate Boundaries
- Sharing Personal Experiences
- Using Self-Talk or Self-Instruction

COMPLEX SKILLS

- Accepting Self
- Asking for Advice
- Being an Appropriate Role Model
- Being Assertive
- Differentiating Friends from Acquaintances
- Displaying Appropriate Control
- Expressing Empathy and Understanding for Others
- Expressing Grief
- Identifying Own Feelings
- Maintaining Relationships
- Recognizing Moods of Others
- Resolving Conflicts
- Taking Risks Appropriately
- Using Self-Monitoring and Self-Reflection

Stereotypic Movement Disorder

Suggested Social Skills Training for Individuals Diagnosed with Stereotypic Movement Disorder

BASIC SKILLS

- Accepting Criticism or a Consequence
- Accepting "No" for an Answer
- Disagreeing Appropriately

INTERMEDIATE SKILLS

- Accepting Consequences
- Accepting Decisions of Authority
- Asking for Help
- Complying with Reasonable Requests
- Getting Another Person's Attention
- Getting the Teacher's Attention
- Making a Request (Asking a Favor)
- Making Positive Self-Statements
- Saying "No" Assertively
- Seeking Positive Attention
- Using Anger Control Strategies
- Using Structured Problem-Solving (SODAS)

ADVANCED SKILLS

- Controlling Emotions
- Coping with Anger and Aggression from Others
- Coping with Change
- Coping with Conflict
- Coping with Sad Feelings (or Depression)
- Dealing with an Accusation
- Dealing with Being Left Out
- Dealing with Boredom
- Dealing with Failure

- Dealing with Fear
- Dealing with Frustration
- Dealing with Rejection
- Expressing Feelings Appropriately
- Preparing for a Stressful Conversation
- Preventing Trouble with Others
- Problem-Solving a Disagreement
- Responding to Complaints
- Responding to Teasing
- Self-Correcting Own Behavior
- Self-Reporting Own Behaviors
- Sharing Attention with Others
- Using Relaxation Strategies
- Using Spontaneous Problem-Solving

COMPLEX SKILLS

- Accepting Self
- Displaying Appropriate Control
- Managing Stress
- Rewarding Yourself
- Seeking Professional Assistance
- Setting Goals
- Using Leisure Time
- Using Self-Monitoring and Self-Reflection

Substance-Related Disorders

ALCOHOL-RELATED DISORDERS

Alcohol Dependence
Alcohol Abuse

AMPHETAMINE-RELATED DISORDERS

Amphetamine Dependence
Amphetamine Abuse

CAFFEINE-RELATED DISORDERS

Caffeine Dependence
Caffeine Abuse

CANNABIS-RELATED DISORDERS

Cannabis Dependence
Cannabis Abuse

COCAINE-RELATED DISORDERS

Cocaine Dependence
Cocaine Abuse

HALLUCINOGEN-RELATED DISORDERS

Hallucinogen Dependence
Hallucinogen Abuse

INHALANT-RELATED DISORDERS

Inhalant Dependence
Inhalant Abuse

NICOTINE-RELATED DISORDERS

Nicotine Dependence
Nicotine Abuse

OPIOID-RELATED DISORDERS

Opioid Dependence
Opioid Abuse

PHENCYCLIDINE-RELATED DISORDERS

Phencyclidine Dependence
Phencyclidine Abuse

SEDATIVE-, HYPNOTIC-, OR ANXIOLYTIC-RELATED DISORDERS

Sedative, Hypnotic, or Anxiolytic Dependence
Sedative, Hypnotic, or Anxiolytic Abuse

POLYSUBSTANCE-RELATED DISORDERS

Polysubstance Dependence
Polysubstance Abuse

OTHER (OR UNKNOWN) SUBSTANCE-RELATED DISORDERS

Other (Or Unknown) Substance Dependence
Other (Or Unknown) Substance Abuse

Suggested Social Skills Training for Individuals Diagnosed with a Substance-Related Disorder

BASIC SKILLS

- Talking with Others

INTERMEDIATE SKILLS

- Asking for Help
- Checking In (or Checking Back)
- Following Rules
- Making Positive Self-Statements
- Participating in Activities
- Refraining from Possessing Contraband or Drugs
- Reporting Emergencies
- Reporting Other Youths' Behavior (or Peer Reporting)
- Resisting Peer Pressure
- Saying "No" Assertively
- Seeking Positive Attention
- Using Structured Problem-Solving (SODAS)

ADVANCED SKILLS

- Accepting Help or Assistance
- Choosing Appropriate Friends
- Communicating Honestly
- Controlling Emotions
- Coping with Anger and Aggression from Others
- Coping with Change
- Coping with Conflict
- Coping with Sad Feelings (or Depression)
- Dealing with an Accusation
- Dealing with Boredom
- Dealing with Failure
- Dealing with Frustration
- Dealing with Group Pressure
- Delaying Gratification
- Expressing Feelings Appropriately
- Expressing Optimism
- Expressing Pride in Accomplishments
- Following Safety Rules
- Making Decisions
- Making Restitution (Compensating)
- Preparing for a Stressful Conversation
- Preventing Trouble with Others
- Problem-Solving a Disagreement
- Self-Correcting Own Behavior
- Self-Reporting Own Behaviors
- Using Relaxation Strategies
- Using Spontaneous Problem-Solving

COMPLEX SKILLS

- Accepting Self
- Altering One's Environment
- Asking for Advice
- Being an Appropriate Role Model
- Being Assertive
- Being Patient
- Clarifying Values and Beliefs
- Differentiating Friends from Acquaintances
- Displaying Appropriate Control
- Identifying Own Feelings
- Laughing at Oneself
- Maintaining Relationships
- Making Moral and Spiritual Decisions

Substance-Related Disorders (Cont)

- Managing Stress
- Rewarding Yourself
- Seeking Professional Assistance
- Setting Goals
- Using Community Resources
- Using Leisure Time
- Using Self-Monitoring and Self-Reflection

Schizophrenia and Other Psychotic Disorders

Schizophrenia
Schizophreniform Disorder
Schizoaffective Disorder

Suggested Social Skills Training for Individuals Diagnosed with Schizophrenia, Schizophreniform Disorder, or Schizoaffective Disorder

BASIC SKILLS

- Accepting Criticism or a Consequence
- Accepting "No" for an Answer
- Disagreeing Appropriately
- Following Instructions
- Introducing Yourself
- Showing Respect
- Showing Sensitivity to Others
- Talking with Others

INTERMEDIATE SKILLS

- Accepting Compliments
- Accepting Consequences
- Asking for Help
- Asking Questions
- Checking In (or Checking Back)
- Choosing Appropriate Words to Say
- Closing a Conversation
- Completing Tasks
- Complying with Reasonable Requests
- Contributing to Discussions (Joining in a Conversation)
- Doing Good Quality Work
- Getting Another Person's Attention

- Greeting Others
- Initiating a Conversation
- Introducing Others
- Listening to Others
- Maintaining a Conversation
- Maintaining an Appropriate Appearance
- Maintaining Personal Hygiene
- Making Positive Self-Statements
- Participating in Activities
- Saying Good-Bye to Guests
- Showing Appreciation
- Showing Interest
- Trying New Tasks
- Using an Appropriate Voice Tone
- Using Structured Problem-Solving (SODAS)

ADVANCED SKILLS

- Accepting Defeat or Loss
- Accepting Help or Assistance
- Advocating for Oneself
- Analyzing Skills Needed for Different Situations

Schizophrenia (Cont)

- Analyzing Social Situations
- Concentrating on a Subject or Task
- Contributing to Group Activities
- Controlling Emotions
- Coping with Change
- Coping with Conflict
- Coping with Sad Feelings (or Depression)
- Dealing with Being Left Out
- Dealing with Boredom
- Dealing with Failure
- Dealing with Fear
- Dealing with Frustration
- Dealing with Rejection
- Displaying Effort
- Expressing Feelings Appropriately
- Expressing Optimism
- Following Safety Rules
- Making Decisions
- Managing Time
- Organizing Tasks and Activities
- Persevering on Tasks and Projects
- Preparing for a Stressful Conversation
- Responding to Teasing
- Self-Correcting Own Behavior
- Self-Reporting Own Behaviors
- Sharing Personal Experiences
- Using Relaxation Strategies
- Using Self-Talk or Self-Instruction
- Using Spontaneous Problem-Solving
- Working Independently

COMPLEX SKILLS

- Accepting Self
- Altering One's Environment
- Asking for Advice
- Assessing Own Abilities
- Budgeting and Managing Money
- Displaying Appropriate Control
- Identifying Own Feelings
- Interviewing for a Job
- Laughing at Oneself
- Maintaining Relationships
- Managing Stress
- Rewarding Yourself
- Seeking Professional Assistance
- Setting Goals
- Using Community Resources
- Using Leisure Time
- Using Self-Monitoring and Self-Reflection
- Using Strategies to Find a Job

Schizoaffective Disorder

Suggested Social Skills Training for Individuals Diagnosed with a Schizoaffective Disorder

BASIC SKILLS

- Accepting Criticism or a Consequence
- Talking with Others

INTERMEDIATE SKILLS

- Accepting Compliments
- Asking for Help
- Completing Tasks
- Conversation Skills
- Doing Good Quality Work
- Following Rules
- Greeting Others
- Interacting with Others
- Interrupting Appropriately
- Maintaining an Appropriate Appearance
- Maintaining Personal Hygiene
- Making a Telephone Call
- Making Positive Self-Statements
- Participating in Activities
- Resisting Peer Pressure
- Saying Good-Bye to Guests
- Saying "No" Assertively
- Seeking Positive Attention
- Showing Appreciation
- Showing Interest
- Staying on Task
- Trying New Tasks
- Using an Appropriate Voice Tone
- Using Anger Control Strategies
- Using Structured Problem-Solving (SODAS)

ADVANCED SKILLS

- Accepting Criticism
- Accepting Defeat or Loss
- Accepting Help or Assistance
- Advocating for Oneself
- Analyzing Skills Needed for Different Situations
- Analyzing Social Situations
- Caring for Others' Property
- Caring for Own Belongings
- Contributing to Group Activities
- Controlling Eating Habits
- Controlling Emotions
- Controlling the Impulse to Lie
- Controlling the Impulse to Steal
- Coping with Change
- Coping with Conflict
- Coping with Sad Feelings (or Depression)
- Dealing with an Accusation
- Dealing with Being Left Out
- Dealing with Boredom
- Dealing with Embarrassing Situations
- Dealing with Failure
- Dealing with Fear
- Dealing with Frustration
- Dealing with Group Pressure
- Dealing with Rejection
- Delaying Gratification
- Displaying Effort
- Expressing Feelings Appropriately
- Expressing Optimism

Schizoaffective Disorder (Cont)

- Expressing Pride in Accomplishments
- Following Safety Rules
- Following Through on Agreements and Contracts
- Interacting Appropriately with Members of the Opposite Sex
- Keeping Property in Its Place
- Making Decisions
- Making New Friends
- Managing Time
- Responding to Others' Humor
- Responding to Teasing
- Self-Correcting Own Behavior
- Self-Reporting Own Behaviors
- Setting Appropriate Boundaries
- Sharing Personal Experiences
- Anger Control Strategies
- Using Relaxation Strategies
- Using Self-Talk or Self-Instruction
- Using Spontaneous Problem-Solving
- Working Independently

- Expressing Grief
- Identifying Own Feelings
- Interviewing for a Job
- Laughing at Oneself
- Maintaining Relationships
- Managing Stress
- Resolving Conflicts
- Rewarding Yourself
- Seeking Professional Assistance
- Setting Goals
- Taking Risks Appropriately
- Using Community Resources
- Using Leisure Time
- Using Self-Monitoring and Self-Reflection

COMPLEX SKILLS

- Accepting Self
- Altering One's Environment
- Asking for Advice
- Assessing Own Abilities
- Being Assertive
- Being Patient
- Budgeting and Managing Money
- Clarifying Values and Beliefs
- Displaying Appropriate Control

Delusional Disorder

Suggested Social Skills Training for Individuals Diagnosed with a Delusional Disorder

BASIC SKILLS

- Accepting Criticism or a Consequence
- Disagreeing Appropriately
- Talking with Others

INTERMEDIATE SKILLS

- Accepting Decisions of Authority
- Asking for Help
- Checking In (Checking Back)
- Choosing Appropriate Words to Say
- Maintaining a Conversation
- Participating in Activities
- Using Structured Problem-Solving (SODAS)

ADVANCED SKILLS

- Analyzing Skills Needed for Different Situations
- Analyzing Social Situations
- Compromising with Others
- Controlling Emotions
- Coping with Anger and Aggression from Others
- Coping with Change
- Coping with Conflict
- Coping with Sad Feelings (or Depression)
- Dealing with Contradictory Messages
- Dealing with Rejection
- Expressing Feelings Appropriately
- Preventing Trouble with Others
- Responding to Teasing
- Self-Correcting Own Behavior

- Self-Reporting Own Behaviors
- Sharing Personal Experiences
- Using Relaxation Strategies
- Using Self-Talk or Self-Instruction
- Using Spontaneous Problem Solving

COMPLEX SKILLS

- Altering One's Environment
- Assessing Own Abilities
- Displaying Appropriate Control
- Identifying Own Feelings
- Laughing at Oneself
- Maintaining Relationships
- Managing Stress
- Seeking Professional Assistance
- Setting Goals
- Using Self-Monitoring and Self-Reflection

Brief Psychotic Disorder
Psychotic Disorder, Not Otherwise Specified

Suggested Social Skills Training for Individuals Diagnosed with Brief Psychotic Disorder or Psychotic Disorder, NOS

BASIC SKILLS

- Talking with Others

INTERMEDIATE SKILLS

- Asking for Help
- Asking Questions
- Checking In (or Checking Back)
- Contributing to Discussions (Joining in a Conversation)
- Getting Another Person's Attention
- Initiating a Conversation
- Listening to Others
- Maintaining a Conversation
- Making Positive Self-Statements
- Participating in Activities

ADVANCED SKILLS

- Accepting Help or Assistance
- Analyzing Skills Needed for Different Situations
- Contributing to Group Activities
- Controlling Emotions
- Coping with Change
- Expressing Feelings Appropriately
- Expressing Optimism
- Preventing Trouble with Others
- Responding to Teasing
- Sharing Personal Experiences
- Using Relaxation Strategies
- Using Self-Talk or Self-Instruction

COMPLEX SKILLS

- Accepting Self
- Altering One's Environment
- Displaying Appropriate Control
- Identifying Own Feelings
- Managing Stress
- Seeking Professional Assistance

Mood Disorders

DEPRESSIVE DISORDERS

Major Depressive Disorder
Dysthymic Disorder
Depressive Disorder, Not Otherwise Specified

Suggested Social Skills Training for Individuals Diagnosed with a Major Depressive Disorder, Dysthymic Disorder, or Depressive Disorder, NOS

BASIC SKILLS

- Talking with Others

INTERMEDIATE SKILLS

- Accepting Compliments
- Asking for Help
- Contributing to Discussions (Joining in a Conversation)
- Doing Good Quality Work
- Greeting Others
- Initiating a Conversation
- Maintaining a Conversation
- Maintaining an Appropriate Appearance
- Maintaining Personal Hygiene
- Making Positive Self-Statements
- Participating in Activities
- Saying Good-Bye to Guests
- Showing Appreciation
- Showing Interest
- Trying New Tasks
- Using Structured Problem-Solving (SODAS)

ADVANCED SKILLS

- Advocating for Oneself
- Analyzing Skills Needed for Different Situations
- Analyzing Social Situations
- Contributing to Group Activities
- Controlling Eating Habits
- Coping with Anger and Aggression from Others
- Coping with Change
- Coping with Conflict
- Coping with Sad Feelings (or Depression)
- Dealing with Being Left Out
- Dealing with Boredom
- Dealing with Embarrassing Situations
- Dealing with Failure
- Dealing with Fear
- Dealing with Frustration
- Dealing with Rejection
- Displaying Effort
- Expressing Feelings Appropriately
- Expressing Optimism

Depressive Disorders (Cont)

- Expressing Pride in Accomplishments
- Making New Friends
- Responding to Others' Humor
- Responding to Teasing
- Self-Correcting Own Behavior
- Using Relaxation Strategies
- Using Self-Talk or Self-Instruction
- Using Spontaneous Problem-Solving

COMPLEX SKILLS

- Accepting Self
- Altering One's Environment
- Asking for Advice
- Being Assertive
- Clarifying Values and Beliefs
- Expressing Grief
- Identifying Own Feelings
- Laughing at Oneself
- Maintaining Relationships
- Managing Stress
- Rewarding Yourself
- Seeking Professional Assistance
- Setting Goals
- Taking Risks Appropriately
- Using Community Resources
- Using Leisure Time
- Using Self-Monitoring and Self-Reflection

Bipolar Disorders

Bipolar I Disorder
Bipolar II Disorder
Cyclothymic Disorder
Bipolar Disorder, Not Otherwise Specified
Mood Disorder, Not Otherwise Specified

Suggested Social Skills Training for Individuals Diagnosed with a Bipolar Disorder or Mood Disorder, NOS

BASIC SKILLS

- Accepting Criticism or a Consequence
- Talking with Others

INTERMEDIATE SKILLS

- Accepting Compliments
- Accepting Help or Assistance
- Advocating for Oneself
- Caring for Others' Property
- Caring for Own Belongings
- Contributing to Discussions (Joining in a Conversation)
- Controlling Emotions
- Controlling the Impulse to Lie
- Controlling the Impulse to Steal
- Coping with Sad Feelings (or Depression)
- Dealing with an Accusation
- Dealing with Boredom
- Dealing with Group Pressure
- Delaying Gratification

- Expressing Feelings Appropriately
- Expressing Optimism
- Expressing Pride in Accomplishments
- Following Rules
- Following Safety Rules
- Following Through on Agreements and Contracts
- Interacting Appropriately with Members of the Opposite Sex
- Keeping Property in Its Place
- Making Decisions
- Making Positive Self-Statements
- Resisting Peer Pressure
- Saying "No" Assertively
- Seeking Positive Attention
- Self-Correcting Own Behavior
- Self-Reporting Own Behaviors
- Sharing Personal Experiences
- Staying on Task
- Using an Appropriate Voice Tone
- Using Anger Control Strategies

Bipolar Disorders (Cont)

- Using Relaxation Strategies
- Using Spontaneous Problem-Solving
- Using Structured Problem-Solving (SODAS)

COMPLEX SKILLS

- Accepting Self
- Assessing Own Abilities
- Being Assertive
- Being Patient
- Budgeting and Managing Money
- Clarifying Values and Beliefs
- Displaying Appropriate Control
- Identifying Own Feelings
- Maintaining Relationships
- Managing Stress
- Resolving Conflicts
- Rewarding Yourself
- Seeking Professional Assistance
- Setting Goals
- Taking Risks Appropriately
- Using Leisure Time
- Using Self-Monitoring and Self-Reflection

Anxiety Disorders

Panic Disorder without Agoraphobia
Panic Disorer with Agoraphobia
Agoraphobia without History of Panic Disorder

Suggested Social Skills Training for Individuals Diagnosed with Panic Disorder with and without Agoraphobia or Agoraphobia without a History of Panic Disorder

BASIC SKILLS

- Disagreeing Appropriately
- Talking with Others

INTERMEDIATE SKILLS

- Accepting Decisions of Authority
- Asking for Help
- Complying with Reasonable Requests
- Making Positive Self-Statements
- Participating in Activities
- Trying New Tasks
- Using Structured Problem-Solving (SODAS)

ADVANCED SKILLS

- Analyzing Skills Needed for Different Situations
- Analyzing Social Situations
- Compromising with Others
- Contributing to Group Activities
- Controlling Emotions
- Coping with Change
- Dealing with Embarrassing Situations

- Dealing with Fear
- Displaying Effort
- Expressing Feelings Appropriately
- Expressing Optimism
- Preparing for a Stressful Conversation
- Using Relaxation Strategies
- Using Self-Talk or Self-Instruction
- Using Spontaneous Problem-Solving

COMPLEX SKILLS

- Assessing Own Abilities
- Displaying Appropriate Control
- Formulating Strategies
- Identifying Own Feelings
- Laughing at Oneself
- Managing Stress
- Rewarding Yourself
- Seeking Professional Assistance
- Setting Goals
- Using Self-Monitoring and Self-Reflection

Specific Phobia

Suggested Social Skills Training for Individuals Diagnosed with a Specific Phobia

BASIC SKILLS

- Talking with Others

INTERMEDIATE SKILLS

- Asking for Help
- Complying with Reasonable Requests
- Making Positive Self-Statements
- Participating in Activities
- Saying "No" Assertively
- Trying New Tasks
- Using Structured Problem-Solving (SODAS)

ADVANCED SKILLS

- Analyzing Skills Needed for Different Situations
- Controlling Emotions
- Dealing with Fear
- Displaying Effort
- Expressing Feelings Appropriately
- Expressing Optimism
- Responding to Teasing
- Using Relaxation Strategies
- Using Self-Talk or Self-Instruction
- Using Spontaneous Problem-Solving

COMPLEX SKILLS

- Altering One's Environment
- Displaying Appropriate Control
- Managing Stress
- Rewarding Yourself
- Seeking Professional Assistance
- Setting Goals
- Taking Risks Appropriately
- Using Self-Monitoring and Self-Reflection

Social Phobia

Suggested Social Skills Training for Individuals Diagnosed with Social Phobia

BASIC SKILLS

- Accepting Criticism or a Consequence
- Introducing Yourself
- Talking with Others

INTERMEDIATE SKILLS

- Accepting Compliments
- Answering the Telephone
- Asking for Help
- Asking Questions
- Choosing Appropriate Words to Say
- Closing a Conversation
- Contributing to Discussions (Joining in a Conversation)
- Correcting Another Person (or Giving Criticism)
- Getting Another Person's Attention
- Getting the Teacher's Attention
- Giving Compliments
- Greeting Others
- Initiating a Conversation
- Interrupting Appropriately
- Introducing Others
- Maintaining a Conversation
- Making a Request (Asking a Favor)
- Making a Telephone Call
- Making Positive Self-Statements
- Making Positive Statements about Others
- Offering Assistance or Help
- Participating in Activities
- Saying Good-Bye to Guests

- Saying "No" Assertively
- Seeking Positive Attention
- Trying New Tasks
- Using Structured Problem-Solving (SODAS)
- Volunteering

ADVANCED SKILLS

- Accepting Defeat or Loss
- Accepting Help or Assistance
- Accepting Winning Appropriately
- Advocating for Oneself
- Analyzing Social Situations
- Choosing Appropriate Friends
- Contributing to Group Activities
- Controlling Emotions
- Coping with Anger and Aggression from Others
- Coping with Change
- Coping with Conflict
- Coping with Sad Feelings (or Depression)
- Dealing with Being Left Out
- Dealing with Embarrassing Situations
- Dealing with Failure
- Dealing with Fear
- Dealing with Group Pressure
- Dealing with Rejection
- Expressing Feelings Appropriately
- Expressing Pride in Accomplishments
- Giving Instructions
- Giving Rationales

Social Phobia (Cont)

- Making New Friends
- Preparing for a Stressful Conversation
- Preventing Trouble with Others
- Problem-Solving a Disagreement
- Responding to Complaints
- Responding to Others' Humor
- Responding to Teasing
- Self-Correcting Own Behavior
- Sharing Personal Experiences
- Suggesting an Activity
- Using Relaxation Strategies
- Using Self-Talk or Self-Instruction

COMPLEX SKILLS

- Accepting Self
- Being Assertive
- Differentiating Friends from Acquaintances
- Identifying Own Feelings
- Interviewing for a Job
- Laughing at Oneself
- Maintaining Relationships
- Managing Stress
- Resolving Conflicts
- Rewarding Yourself
- Seeking Professional Assistance
- Setting Goals
- Taking Risks Appropriately
- Using Self-Monitoring and Self-Reflection

Obsessive-Compulsive Disorder

Suggested Social Skills Training for Individuals Diagnosed with Obsessive-Compulsive Disorder

BASIC SKILLS

- Accepting Criticism or a Consequence
- Accepting "No" for an Answer
- Talking with Others

INTERMEDIATE SKILLS

- Accepting Decisions of Authority
- Asking for Help
- Complying with Reasonable Requests
- Making Positive Self-Statements
- Participating in Activities
- Trying New Tasks
- Using Structured Problem-Solving (SODAS)

ADVANCED SKILLS

- Compromising with Others
- Controlling Emotions
- Coping with Change
- Coping with Conflict
- Dealing with Boredom
- Dealing with Failure
- Dealing with Fear
- Dealing with Frustration
- Delaying Gratification
- Expressing Feelings Appropriately
- Responding to Teasing
- Self-Correcting Own Behavior
- Self-Reporting Own Behaviors
- Using Relaxation Strategies
- Using Self-Talk or Self-Instruction
- Using Spontaneous Problem-Solving

COMPLEX SKILLS

- Accepting Self
- Altering One's Environment
- Being Patient
- Displaying Appropriate Control
- Identifying Own Feelings
- Laughing at Oneself
- Maintaining Relationships
- Managing Stress
- Rewarding Yourself
- Seeking Professional Assistance
- Setting Goals
- Taking Risks Appropriately
- Using Leisure Time
- Using Self-Monitoring and Self-Reflection

Posttraumatic Stress Disorder
Acute Stress Disorder

Suggested Social Skills Training for Individuals Diagnosed with Posttraumatic Stress Disorder or Acute Stress Disorder

BASIC SKILLS

- Talking with Others

INTERMEDIATE SKILLS

- Accepting Apologies from Others
- Accepting Compliments
- Asking for Help
- Contributing to Discussions (Joining in a Conversation)
- Greeting Others
- Initiating a Conversation
- Maintaining a Conversation
- Maintaining an Appropriate Appearance
- Maintaining Personal Hygiene
- Making Positive Self-Statements
- Participating in Activities
- Resisting Peer Pressure
- Saying "No" Assertively
- Seeking Positive Attention
- Using Structured Problem-Solving (SODAS)

ADVANCED SKILLS

- Accepting Defeat or Loss
- Accepting Help or Assistance
- Advocating for Oneself
- Analyzing Skills Needed for Different Situations

- Analyzing Social Situations
- Concentrating on a Subject or Task
- Contributing to Group Activities
- Controlling Emotions
- Controlling Sexually Abusive Impulses toward Others
- Coping with Anger and Aggression from Others
- Coping with Change
- Coping with Conflict
- Coping with Sad Feelings (or Depression)
- Dealing with Fear
- Dealing with Frustration
- Dealing with Group Pressure
- Displaying Effort
- Expressing Appropriate Affection
- Expressing Feelings Appropriately
- Expressing Optimism
- Expressing Pride in Accomplishments
- Interacting Appropriately with the Opposite Sex
- Making Decisions
- Making New Friends
- Preparing for a Stressful Conversation
- Self-Correcting Own Behavior
- Self-Reporting Own Behaviors
- Setting Appropriate Boundaries
- Sharing Personnel Experiences

Posttraumatic Stress Disorder (Cont)

- Using Relaxation Strategies
- Using Self-Talk or Self-Instruction
- Using Spontaneous
  Problem-Solving

COMPLEX SKILLS

- Accepting Self
- Altering One's Environment
- Asking for Advice
- Being Assertive
- Clarifying Values and Beliefs
- Differentiating Friends from
  Acquaintances
- Displaying Appropriate Control
- Identifying Own Feelings
- Laughing at Oneself
- Maintaining Relationships
- Managing Stress
- Rewarding Yourself
- Seeking Professional Assistance
- Setting Goals
- Taking Risks Appropriately
- Using Leisure Time
- Using Self-Monitoring and
  Self-Reflection

Generalized Anxiety Disorder
Anxiety Disorder, Not Otherwise Specified

Suggested Social Skills Training for Individuals Diagnosed with Generalized Anxiety Disorder or Anxiety Disorder, NOS

BASIC SKILLS

- Talking with Others

INTERMEDIATE SKILLS

- Asking for Help
- Complying with Reasonable Requests
- Making Positive Self-Statements
- Participating in Activities
- Trying New Tasks
- Using Structured Problem-Solving (SODAS)

ADVANCED SKILLS

- Analyzing Skills Needed for Different Situations
- Analyzing Social Situations
- Concentrating on a Subject or Task
- Controlling Emotions
- Coping with Anger and Aggression from Others
- Coping with Conflict
- Coping with Sad Feelings (or Depression)
- Dealing with an Accusation
- Dealing with Being Left Out
- Dealing with Boredom
- Dealing with Contradictory Messages
- Dealing with Embarrassing Situations
- Dealing with Failure
- Dealing with Fear

- Dealing with Frustration
- Dealing with Group Pressure
- Dealing with Rejection
- Expressing Feelings Appropriately
- Expressing Optimism
- Using Relaxation Strategies
- Using Self-Talk or Self-Instruction
- Using Spontaneous Problem-Solving

COMPLEX SKILLS

- Accepting Self
- Altering One's Environment
- Clarifying Values and Beliefs
- Displaying Appropriate Control
- Laughing at Oneself
- Managing Stress
- Rewarding Yourself
- Seeking Professional Assistance
- Setting Goals
- Taking Risks Appropriately
- Using Self-Monitoring and Self-Reflection

Somatoform Disorders

Somatization Disorder
Undifferentiated Somatoform Disorder
Conversion Disorder

Suggested Social Skills Training for Individuals Diagnosed with Somatization Disorder, Undifferentiated Somatoform Disorder, or Conversion Disorder

BASIC SKILLS

- Talking with Others

INTERMEDIATE SKILLS

- Accepting Decisions of Authority
- Asking for Help
- Asking Questions
- Completing Tasks
- Complying with Reasonable Requests
- Contributing to Discussions (Joining in a Conversation)
- Doing Good Quality Work
- Getting Another Person's Attention
- Greeting Others
- Initiating a Conversation
- Interrupting Appropriately
- Listening to Others
- Maintaining a Conversation
- Maintaining an Appropriate Appearance
- Maintaining Personal Hygiene
- Making Positive Self-Statements
- Participating in Activities
- Saying Good-Bye to Guests
- Seeking Positive Attention
- Showing Appreciation
- Showing Interest
- Using an Appropriate Voice Tone
- Using Anger Control Strategies
- Using Structured Problem-Solving (SODAS)

ADVANCED SKILLS

- Concentrating on a Subject or Task
- Contributing to Group Activities
- Controlling Emotions
- Cooperating with Others
- Coping with Change
- Coping with Conflict
- Coping with Sad Feelings (or Depression)
- Dealing with Fear
- Dealing with Frustration
- Displaying Effort
- Expressing Feelings Appropriately
- Expressing Optimism

Somatoform Disorders (Cont)

- Persevering on Tasks and Activities
- Organizing Tasks and Activities
- Responding to Others' Feelings
- Self-Correcting Own Behavior
- Setting Appropriate Boundaries
- Sharing Personal Experiences
- Using Relaxation Strategies
- Using Self-Talk or Self-Instruction
- Using Spontaneous Problem-Solving
- Working Independently

COMPLEX SKILLS

- Accepting Self
- Altering One's Environment
- Assessing Own Abilities
- Being Patient
- Displaying Appropriate Control
- Expressing Empathy and Understanding for Others
- Identifying Own Feelings
- Laughing at Oneself
- Maintaining Relationships
- Managing Stress
- Resolving Conflicts
- Rewarding Yourself
- Seeking Professional Assistance
- Using Self-Monitoring and Self-Reflection

Pain Disorder

Suggested Social Skills Training for Individuals Diagnosed with Pain Disorder

BASIC SKILLS

- Talking with Others

INTERMEDIATE SKILLS

- Asking for Help
- Asking Questions
- Listening to Others
- Making Positive Self-Statements
- Participating in Activities
- Using Anger Control Strategies
- Using Structured Problem-Solving (SODAS)

ADVANCED SKILLS

- Accepting Defeat or Loss
- Accepting Help or Assistance
- Advocating for Oneself
- Controlling Emotions
- Coping with Change
- Coping with Conflict
- Coping with Others' Negative Emotions
- Coping with Sad Feelings (or Depression)
- Dealing with Fear
- Dealing with Frustration
- Expressing Feelings Appropriately
- Expressing Optimism
- Making Decisions
- Making Restitution
- Organizing Tasks and Activities
- Responding to Complaints
- Responding to Others' Feelings

- Self-Correcting Own Behavior
- Setting Appropriate Boundaries
- Sharing Personal Experiences
- Using Relaxation Strategies
- Using Spontaneous Problem-Solving

COMPLEX SKILLS

- Accepting Self
- Assessing Own Abilities
- Being Assertive
- Displaying Appropriate Control
- Expressing Empathy and Understanding for Others
- Expressing Grief
- Laughing at Oneself
- Managing Stress
- Resolving Conflict
- Seeking Professional Assistance
- Using Self-Monitoring and Self-Reflection

Hypochondriasis

Suggested Social Skills Training for Individuals Diagnosed with Hypochondriasis

BASIC SKILLS

- Talking with Others

INTERMEDIATE SKILLS

- Accepting Decisions of Authority
- Making Positive Self-Statements
- Participating in Activities

ADVANCED SKILLS

- Controlling Emotions
- Dealing with Contradictory Messages
- Dealing with Fear
- Expressing Optimism
- Sharing Personal Experiences
- Using Relaxation Strategies
- Using Self-Talk or Self-Instruction

COMPLEX SKILLS

- Laughing at Oneself
- Managing Stress
- Seeking Professional Assistance
- Using Self-Monitoring and Self-Reflection

Body Dysmorphic Disorder

Suggested Social Skills for Individuals Diagnosed with Body Dysmorphic Disorder

BASIC SKILLS

- Talking with Others

INTERMEDIATE SKILLS

- Accepting Compliments
- Making Positive Self-Statements
- Participating in Activities

ADVANCED SKILLS

- Advocating for Oneself
- Choosing Appropriate Clothing
- Controlling Emotions
- Coping with Sad Feelings
  (or Depression)
- Dealing with Embarrassing Situations
- Expressing Feelings Appropriately
- Expressing Optimism
- Expressing Pride in Accomplishments
- Responding to Others' Humor
- Responding to Teasing
- Using Self-Talk or Self-Instruction

COMPLEX SKILLS

- Accepting Self
- Being Assertive
- Clarifying Values and Beliefs
- Identifying Own Feelings
- Laughing at Oneself
- Using Self-Monitoring and
  Self-Reflection

Somatoform Disorder, Not Otherwise Specified

Suggested Social Skills Training for Individuals Diagnosed with Somatoform Disorder, NOS

BASIC SKILLS

- Talking with Others

INTERMEDIATE SKILLS

- Asking for Help
- Making Positive Self-Statements
- Participating in Activities
- Seeking Positive Attention
- Using Structured Problem-Solving (SODAS)

ADVANCED SKILLS

- Contributing to Group Activities
- Controlling Emotions
- Coping with Change
- Coping with Conflict
- Coping with Sad Feelings (or Depression)
- Dealing with Embarrassing Situations
- Dealing with Failure
- Dealing with Fear
- Dealing with Frustration
- Dealing with Rejection
- Displaying Effort
- Expressing Feelings Appropriately
- Expressing Optimism
- Preparing for a Stressful Conversation
- Problem-Solving a Disagreement
- Self-Correcting Own Behavior
- Using Relaxation Strategies

- Using Self-Talk or Self-Instruction
- Using Spontaneous Problem-Solving

COMPLEX SKILLS

- Accepting Self
- Altering One's Environment
- Displaying Appropriate Control
- Identifying Own Feelings
- Laughing at Oneself
- Managing Stress
- Seeking Professional Assistance
- Setting Goals

Factitious Disorders

Factitious Disorder
Factitious Disorder, Not Otherwise Specified

Suggested Social Skills Training for Individuals Diagnosed with Factitious Disorder or Factitious Disorder, NOS

BASIC SKILLS

- Talking with Others

INTERMEDIATE SKILLS

- Asking for Help
- Getting Another Person's Attention
- Getting the Teacher's Attention
- Initiating a Conversation
- Maintaining a Conversation
- Maintaining an Appropriate Appearance
- Maintaining Personal Hygiene
- Making a Request (Asking a Favor)
- Making Positive Self-Statements
- Seeking Positive Attention
- Using Structured Problem-Solving (SODAS)

ADVANCED SKILLS

- Analyzing Skills Needed for Different Situations
- Communicating Honestly
- Controlling the Impulse to Lie
- Coping with Sad Feelings (or Depression)
- Dealing with Being Left Out
- Dealing with Boredom
- Dealing with Rejection
- Expressing Feelings Appropriately
- Making New Friends
- Self-Correcting Own Behavior
- Self-Reporting Own Behaviors
- Sharing Attention with Others
- Using Self-Talk or Self-Instruction
- Using Spontaneous Problem-Solving
- Working Independently

COMPLEX SKILLS

- Accepting Self
- Clarifying Values and Beliefs
- Identifying Own Feelings
- Maintaining Relationships
- Rewarding Yourself
- Setting Goals
- Using Self-Monitoring and Self-Reflection

Dissociative Disorders

Dissociative Amnesia
Dissociative Fugue
Dissociative Identity Disorder
Depersonalization Disorder
Dissociative Disorder, Not Otherwise Specified

Suggested Social Skills Training for Individuals Diagnosed with a Dissociative Disorder

BASIC SKILLS
- Talking with Others

INTERMEDIATE SKILLS
- Asking for Help
- Participating in Activities

ADVANCED SKILLS
- Accepting Help or Assistance
- Analyzing Skills Needed for Different Situations
- Coping with Anger and Aggression from Others
- Coping with Change
- Coping with Conflict
- Coping with Sad Feelings (or Depression)
- Dealing with Fear
- Expressing Feelings Appropriately
- Preparing for a Stressful Conversation
- Self-Reporting Own Behaviors
- Using Relaxation Strategies
- Using Spontaneous Problem-Solving

COMPLEX SKILLS
- Accepting Self
- Altering One's Environment
- Identifying Own Feelings
- Managing Stress
- Seeking Professional Assistance
- Setting Goals
- Taking Risks Appropriately
- Using Self-Monitoring and Self-Reflection

Eating Disorders

Anorexia Nervosa
Bulimia Nervosa
Eating Disorder, Not Otherwise Specified

Suggested Social Skills Training for Individuals Diagnosed with Anorexia Nervosa, Bulimia Nervosa, or Eating Disorder, NOS

BASIC SKILLS
- Talking with Others

INTERMEDIATE SKILLS
- Asking for Help
- Making Positive Self-Statements
- Using Structured Problem-Solving (SODAS)

ADVANCED SKILLS
- Choosing Appropriate Clothing
- Communicating Honestly
- Controlling Eating Habits
- Coping with Anger and Aggression from Others
- Coping with Conflict
- Coping with Sad Feelings (or Depression)
- Expressing Feelings Appropriately
- Expressing Optimism
- Expressing Pride in Accomplishments
- Planning Meals
- Preparing for a Stressful Conversation
- Problem-Solving a Disagreement

- Self-Correcting Own Behavior
- Self-Reporting Own Behaviors
- Using Relaxation Strategies
- Using Self-Talk or Self-Instruction
- Using Spontaneous Problem-Solving

COMPLEX SKILLS
- Accepting Self
- Altering One's Environment
- Clarifying Values and Beliefs
- Identifying Own Feelings
- Managing Stress
- Resolving Conflicts
- Rewarding Yourself
- Seeking Professional Assistance
- Setting Goals
- Using Leisure Time
- Using Self-Monitoring and Self-Reflection

Impulse-Control Disorders Not Classified Elsewhere

Intermittent Explosive Disorder

Suggested Social Skills Training for Individuals Diagnosed with Intermittent Explosive Disorder

BASIC SKILLS

- Accepting Criticism or a Consequence
- Accepting "No" for an Answer
- Disagreeing Appropriately
- Showing Respect
- Showing Sensitivity to Others
- Talking with Others

INTERMEDIATE SKILLS

- Accepting Consequences
- Accepting Decisions of Authority
- Asking for Clarification
- Choosing Appropriate Words to Say
- Correcting Another Person (or Giving Criticism)
- Ignoring Distractions by Others
- Interrupting Appropriately
- Listening to Others
- Making an Apology
- Saying "No" Assertively
- Using an Appropriate Voice Tone
- Using Anger Control Strategies
- Using Structured Problem Solving (SODAS)
- Waiting Your Turn

ADVANCED SKILLS GROUP

- Accepting Defeat or Loss
- Analyzing Skills Needed for Different Situations
- Analyzing Social Situations
- Caring for Others' Property
- Caring for Own Belongings
- Compromising with Others
- Controlling Emotions
- Cooperating with Others
- Coping with Anger and Aggression from Others
- Coping with Change
- Coping with Conflict
- Dealing with an Accusation
- Dealing with Being Left Out
- Dealing with Boredom
- Dealing with Contradictory Messages
- Dealing with Embarrassing Situations
- Dealing with Failure
- Dealing with Frustration
- Dealing with Rejection
- Delaying Gratification
- Displaying Sportsmanship
- Expressing Feelings Appropriately
- Making Restitution (Compensating)

Intermittent Explosive Disorder (Cont)

- Negotiating with Others
- Persevering on Tasks and Projects
- Preparing for a Stressful Conversation
- Preventing Trouble with Others
- Problem-Solving a Disagreement
- Responding to Complaints
- Responding to Others' Humor
- Responding to Teasing
- Self-Correcting Own Behavior
- Self-Reporting Own Behaviors
- Setting Appropriate Boundaries
- Using Appropriate Language
- Using Relaxation Strategies
- Using Self-Talk or Self-Instruction
- Using Spontaneous Problem-Solving

COMPLEX SKILLS

- Altering One's Environment
- Being an Appropriate Role Model
- Being Assertive
- Being Patient
- Displaying Appropriate Control
- Identifying Own Feelings
- Laughing at Oneself
- Managing Stress
- Resolving Conflicts
- Rewarding Yourself
- Setting Goals
- Tolerating Differences
- Using Self-Monitoring and Self-Reflection

Kleptomania

Suggested Social Skills Training for Individuals Diagnosed with Kleptomania

BASIC SKILLS

- Accepting "No" for an Answer
- Showing Respect
- Showing Sensitivity to Others
- Talking with Others

INTERMEDIATE SKILLS

- Checking In (or Checking Back)
- Following Rules
- Making an Apology
- Resisting Peer Pressure
- Using Structured Problem-Solving (SODAS)

ADVANCED SKILLS

- Borrowing from Others
- Caring for Others' Property
- Choosing Appropriate Friends
- Communicating Honestly
- Controlling the Impulse to Lie
- Controlling the Impulse to Steal
- Dealing with an Accusation
- Delaying Gratification
- Keeping Property in Its Place
- Making Decisions
- Making Restitution (Compensating)
- Self-Correcting Own Behavior
- Self-Reporting Own Behaviors
- Using Self-Talk or Self-Instruction
- Using Spontaneous Problem-Solving

COMPLEX SKILLS

- Altering One's Environment
- Being an Appropriate Role Model
- Displaying Appropriate Control
- Expressing Empathy and Understanding for Others
- Setting Goals
- Using Leisure Time
- Using Self-Monitoring and Self-Reflection

Pyromania

Suggested Social Skills Training for Individuals Diagnosed with Pyromania

BASIC SKILLS

- Accepting Criticism or a Consequence
- Accepting "No" for an Answer
- Following Instructions
- Showing Respect
- Showing Sensitivity to Others
- Talking with Others

INTERMEDIATE SKILLS

- Accepting Consequences
- Accepting Decisions of Authority
- Asking for Help
- Checking In (or Checking Back)
- Contributing to Discussions (Joining in a Discussion)
- Following Rules
- Getting Another Person's Attention
- Greeting Others
- Initiating a Conversation
- Maintaining a Conversation
- Participating in Activities
- Reporting Emergencies
- Reporting Other Youths' Behavior (or Peer Reporting)
- Saying "No" Assertively
- Seeking Positive Attention
- Using Structured Problem-Solving (SODAS)

ADVANCED SKILLS

- Caring for Others' Property
- Caring for Own Belongings
- Choosing Appropriate Friends
- Communicating Honestly
- Controlling Emotions
- Coping with Anger and Aggression from Others
- Dealing with an Accusation
- Dealing with Boredom
- Dealing with Frustration
- Dealing with Group Pressure
- Delaying Gratification
- Expressing Feelings Appropriately
- Following Safety Rules
- Following Through on Agreements and Contracts
- Making Decisions
- Making Restitution (Compensating)
- Preventing Trouble with Others
- Responding to Others' Feelings
- Self-Correcting Own Behavior
- Self-Reporting Own Behaviors
- Using Relaxation Strategies
- Using Self-Talk or Self-Instruction
- Using Spontaneous Problem-Solving

Pyromania (Cont)

COMPLEX SKILLS

- Accepting Self
- Altering One's Environment
- Being an Appropriate Role Model
- Being Assertive
- Displaying Appropriate Control
- Expressing Empathy and Understanding for Others
- Identifying Own Feelings
- Maintaining Relationships
- Managing Stress
- Resolving Conflicts
- Seeking Professional Assistance
- Using Leisure Time
- Using Self-Monitoring and Self-Reflection

Pathological Gambling

Suggested Social Skills Training for Individuals Diagnosed with Pathological Gambling

BASIC SKILLS

- Accepting "No" for an Answer
- Accepting Criticism or a Consequence
- Disagreeing Appropriately
- Following Instructions
- Showing Respect
- Showing Sensitivity to Others

INTERMEDIATE SKILLS

- Accepting Consequences
- Accepting Decisions of Authority
- Asking for Help
- Complying with Reasonable Requests
- Following Rules
- Greeting Others
- Listening to Others
- Making an Apology
- Making Positive Self-Statements
- Resisting Peer Pressure
- Saying "No" Assertively
- Seeking Positive Attention
- Showing Appreciation
- Staying on Task
- Using Anger Control Strategies
- Using Structured Problem-Solving (SODAS)

ADVANCED SKILLS

- Accepting Defeat or Loss
- Accepting Help or Assistance
- Communicating Honestly

- Controlling Emotions
- Controlling the Impulse to Lie
- Controlling the Impulse to Steal
- Coping with Anger
- Coping with Conflict
- Coping with Sad Feelings (or Depression)
- Dealing with an Accusation
- Dealing with Frustration
- Delaying Gratification
- Expressing Feelings Appropriately
- Expressing Optimism
- Making Decisions
- Managing Time
- Preventing Trouble with Others
- Responding to Complaints
- Responding to Others' Feelings
- Self-Correcting Own Behavior
- Self-Reporting Own Behaviors
- Setting Appropriate Boundaries
- Using Self-Talk or Self-Instruction
- Using Spontaneous Problem-Solving

COMPLEX SKILLS

- Accepting Self
- Altering One's Environment
- Being Assertive
- Budgeting and Managing Money
- Displaying Appropriate Control
- Maintaining Relationships
- Setting Goals

Pathological Gambling (Cont)

- Taking Risks Appropriately
- Using Leisure Time Appropriately
- Using Self-Monitoring and Self-Reflection

Trichotillomania

Suggested Social Skills Training for Individuals Diagnosed with Trichotillomania

BASIC SKILLS

- Accepting Criticism or a Consequence
- Talking with Others

INTERMEDIATE SKILLS

- Accepting Consequences
- Asking for Help
- Contributing to Discussions (Joining in a Conversation)
- Making Positive Self-Statements
- Participating in Activities
- Using Structured Problem-Solving (SODAS)

ADVANCED SKILLS

- Controlling Emotions
- Coping with Change
- Coping with Conflict
- Coping with Sad Feelings (or Depression)
- Dealing with Boredom
- Dealing with Embarrassing Situations
- Dealing with Failure
- Dealing with Frustration
- Dealing with Rejection
- Delaying Gratification
- Expressing Feelings Appropriately
- Expressing Pride in Accomplishments
- Following Through on Agreements and Contracts
- Responding to Teasing
- Self-Correcting Own Behavior

- Self-Reporting Own Behaviors
- Using Relaxation Strategies
- Using Self-Talk or Self-Instruction

COMPLEX SKILLS

- Accepting Self
- Altering One's Environment
- Displaying Appropriate Control
- Formulating Strategies
- Identifying Own Feelings
- Laughing at Oneself
- Maintaining Relationships
- Managing Stress
- Rewarding Yourself
- Seeking Professional Assistance
- Setting Goals
- Using Leisure Time
- Using Self-Monitoring and Self-Reflection

Impulse-Control Disorder, Not Otherwise Specified

Suggested Social Skills Training for Individuals Diagnosed with Impulse-Control Disorder, NOS

BASIC SKILLS

- Talking with Others

INTERMEDIATE SKILLS

- Using Structured Problem Solving (SODAS)

ADVANCED SKILLS GROUP

- Analyzing Skills Needed for Different Situations
- Analyzing Social Situations
- Controlling Emotions
- Coping with Anger and Aggression from Others
- Coping with Change
- Coping with Conflict
- Coping with Sad Feelings (or Depression)
- Dealing with an Accusation
- Dealing with Being Left Out
- Dealing with Boredom
- Dealing with Contradictory Messages
- Dealing with Embarrassing Situations
- Dealing with Failure
- Dealing with Fear
- Dealing with Frustration
- Dealing with Rejection
- Delaying Gratification
- Expressing Feelings Appropriately
- Preparing for a Stressful Conversation

- Problem-Solving a Disagreement
- Responding to Teasing
- Self-Correcting Own Behavior
- Self-Reporting Own Behaviors
- Using Relaxation Strategies
- Using Self-Talk or Self-Instruction
- Using Spontaneous Problem-Solving

COMPLEX SKILLS

- Altering One's Environment
- Displaying Appropriate Control
- Identifying Own Feelings
- Managing Stress
- Rewarding Yourself
- Setting Goals
- Using Self-Monitoring and Self-Reflection

Adjustment Disorders

Adjustment Disorder

Suggested Social Skills Training for Individuals Diagnosed with Adjustment Disorders

BASIC SKILLS

- Accepting Criticism or a Consequence
- Disagreeing Appropriately
- Talking with Others

INTERMEDIATE SKILLS

- Accepting Apologies from Others
- Asking for Help
- Asking Questions
- Contributing to Discussions (Joining in a Conversation)
- Initiating a Conversation
- Maintaining a Conversation
- Making Positive Self-Statements
- Making Positive Statements about Others
- Participating in Activities
- Saying "No" Assertively
- Using Anger Control Strategies
- Using Structured Problem-Solving (SODAS)

ADVANCED SKILLS

- Accepting Defeat or Loss
- Accepting Help or Assistance
- Advocating for Oneself
- Communicating Honestly

- Contributing to Group Activities
- Controlling Emotions
- Controlling the Impulse to Lie
- Cooperating with Others
- Coping with Anger and Aggression from Others
- Coping with Change
- Coping with Conflict
- Coping with Sad Feelings (or Depression)
- Dealing with Embarrassing Situations
- Dealing with Failure
- Dealing with Fear
- Dealing with Frustration
- Displaying Effort
- Displaying Sportsmanship
- Expressing Appropriate Affection
- Expressing Feelings Appropriately
- Expressing Optimism
- Expressing Pride in Accomplishments
- Making Decisions
- Making New Friends
- Negotiating with Others
- Preparing for a Stressful Conversation
- Preventing Trouble with Others
- Problem-Solving a Disagreement
- Responding to Complaints

Adjustment Disorder (Cont)

- Responding to Others' Feelings
- Responding to Others' Humor
- Responding to Teasing
- Self-Correcting Own Behavior
- Self-Reporting Own Behaviors
- Setting Appropriate Boundaries
- Sharing Attention with Others
- Sharing Personal Experiences
- Using Relaxation Strategies
- Using Self-Talk or Self-Instruction
- Using Spontaneous Problem-Solving

- Setting Goals
- Using Self-Monitoring and Self-Reflection

COMPLEX SKILLS

- Accepting Self
- Altering One's Environment
- Asking for Advice
- Being an Appropriate Role Model
- Being Assertive
- Being Patient
- Clarifying Values and Beliefs
- Displaying Appropriate Control
- Expressing Grief
- Formulating Strategies
- Identifying Own Feelings
- Laughing at Oneself
- Maintaining Relationships
- Making an Appropriate Complaint
- Managing Stress
- Resolving Conflicts
- Rewarding Yourself
- Seeking Professional Assistance

Personality Disorders

CLUSTER A PERSONALITY DISORDERS
Paranoid Personality Disorder

Suggested Social Skills Training for Individuals Diagnosed with Paranoid Personality Disorder

BASIC SKILLS

- Accepting Criticism or a Consequence
- Disagreeing Appropriately
- Introducing Yourself
- Talking with Others

INTERMEDIATE SKILLS

- Accepting Compliments
- Accepting Consequences
- Accepting Decisions of Authority
- Asking for Help
- Choosing Appropriate Words to Say
- Closing a Conversation
- Complying with Reasonable Requests
- Contributing to Discussions (Joining in a Conversation)
- Greeting Others
- Initiating a Conversation
- Interrupting Appropriately
- Introducing Others
- Listening to Others
- Maintaining a Conversation
- Maintaining Appropriate Appearance
- Maintaining Personal Hygiene
- Making Positive Self-Statements
- Making Positive Statements about Others
- Participating in Activities
- Saying Good-Bye to Guests
- Seeking Positive Attention
- Trying New Tasks
- Using Structured Problem-Solving (SODAS)

ADVANCED SKILLS

- Accepting Help or Assistance
- Analyzing Social Situations
- Compromising with Others
- Contributing to Group Activities
- Coping with Change
- Coping with Conflict
- Dealing with Contradictory Messages
- Dealing with Fear
- Dealing with Frustration
- Dealing with Rejection
- Expressing Feelings Appropriately
- Expressing Optimism
- Making New Friends

Paranoid Personality Disorder (Cont)

- Responding to Teasing
- Self-Correcting Own Behavior
- Self-Reporting Own Behaviors
- Sharing Personal Experiences
- Using Relaxation Strategies
- Using Self-Talk or Self-Instruction
- Using Spontaneous Problem-Solving

COMPLEX SKILLS

- Altering One's Environment
- Asking for Advice
- Identifying Own Feelings
- Interviewing for a Job
- Laughing at Oneself
- Maintaining Relationships
- Seeking Professional Assistance
- Tolerating Differences
- Using Self-Monitoring and Self-Reflection

Schizoid Personality Disorder

Suggested Social Skills Training for Individuals Diagnosed with Schizoid Personality Disorder

BASIC SKILLS

- Talking with Others
- Introducing Yourself
- Accepting Criticism or a Consequence
- Disagreeing Appropriately
- Showing Sensitivity to Others

INTERMEDIATE SKILLS

- Accepting Compliments
- Accepting Consequences
- Accepting Decisions of Authority
- Asking for Help
- Choosing Appropriate Words to Say
- Closing a Conversation
- Contributing to Discussions (Joining in a Conversation)
- Getting Another Person's Attention
- Giving Compliments
- Greeting Others
- Initiating a Conversation
- Interrupting Appropriately
- Introducing Others
- Listening to Others
- Maintaining a Conversation
- Maintaining Appropriate Appearance
- Maintaining Personal Hygiene
- Making Positive Self-Statements
- Making Positive Statements about Others

- Participating in Activities
- Saying Good-Bye to Guests
- Seeking Positive Attention
- Showing Appreciation
- Showing Interest
- Trying New Tasks
- Using an Appropriate Voice Tone
- Using Structured Problem-Solving (SODAS)

ADVANCED SKILLS

- Accepting Help or Assistance
- Analyzing Social Situations
- Compromising with Others
- Contributing to Group Activities
- Coping with Change
- Dealing with Rejection
- Expressing Appropriate Affection
- Expressing Feelings Appropriately
- Expressing Optimism
- Making New Friends
- Responding to Others' Feelings
- Responding to Others' Humor
- Responding to Teasing
- Self-Correcting Own Behavior
- Suggesting an Activity
- Using Relaxation Strategies
- Using Self-Talk or Self-Instruction
- Using Spontaneous Problem-Solving

Schizoid Personality Disorder (Cont)

COMPLEX SKILLS

- Asking for Advice
- Expressing Empathy and Understanding for Others
- Identifying Own Feelings
- Maintaining Relationships
- Recognizing Moods of Others
- Resolving Conflicts
- Seeking Professional Assistance
- Tolerating Differences
- Using Self-Monitoring and Self-Reflection

Schizotypal Personality Disorder

Suggested Social Skills Training for Individuals Diagnosed with Schizotypal Personality Disorder

BASIC SKILLS

- Accepting Criticism or a Consequence
- Disagreeing Appropriately
- Showing Sensitivity to Others
- Talking with Others

INTERMEDIATE SKILLS

- Accepting Consequences
- Accepting Decisions of Authority
- Choosing Appropriate Words to Say
- Closing a Conversation
- Complying with Reasonable Requests
- Contributing to Discussions (Joining in a Conversation)
- Getting Another Person's Attention
- Giving Compliments
- Greeting Others
- Initiating a Conversation
- Interrupting Appropriately
- Introducing Others
- Listening to Others
- Maintaining a Conversation
- Maintaining Appropriate Appearance
- Participating in Activities
- Saying Good-Bye to Guests
- Seeking Positive Attention
- Using an Appropriate Voice Tone
- Using Structured Problem-Solving (SODAS)

ADVANCED SKILLS

- Analyzing Skills Needed for Different Situations
- Analyzing Social Situations

- Compromising with Others
- Contributing to Group Activities
- Coping with Change
- Dealing with Fear
- Dealing with Frustration
- Dealing with Rejection
- Expressing Feelings Appropriately
- Making New Friends
- Responding to Teasing
- Self-Correcting Own Behavior
- Sharing Personal Experiences
- Suggesting an Activity
- Using Relaxation Strategies
- Using Self-Talk or Self-Instruction
- Using Spontaneous Problem-Solving

COMPLEX SKILLS

- Accepting Self
- Asking for Advice
- Assessing Own Abilities
- Displaying Appropriate Control
- Identifying Own Feelings
- Interviewing for a Job
- Laughing at Oneself
- Maintaining Relationships
- Recognizing Moods of Others
- Seeking Professional Assistance
- Using Self-Monitoring and Self-Reflection

CLUSTER B PERSONALITY DISORDERS
Antisocial Personality Disorder

Suggested Social Skills Training for Individuals Diagnosed with Antisocial Personality Disorder

BASIC SKILLS
- Accepting Criticism or a Consequence
- Accepting "No" for an Answer
- Disagreeing Appropriately
- Following Instructions
- Showing Respect
- Showing Sensitivity to Others

INTERMEDIATE SKILLS
- Accepting Consequences
- Accepting Decisions of Authority
- Checking In (or Checking Back)
- Choosing Appropriate Words to Say
- Closing a Conversation
- Complying with Reasonable Requests
- Contributing to Discussions (Joining in a Conversation)
- Following Rules
- Getting Another Person's Attention
- Giving Compliments
- Greeting Others
- Initiating a Conversation
- Interrupting Appropriately
- Introducing Others
- Listening to Others
- Maintaining a Conversation
- Making an Apology
- Making Positive Statements about Others
- Offering Assistance or Help

- Participating in Activities
- Refraining from Possessing Contraband or Drugs
- Reporting Emergencies
- Resisting Peer Pressure
- Saying Good-Bye to Guests
- Saying "No" Assertively
- Seeking Positive Attention
- Showing Appreciation
- Using an Appropriate Voice Tone
- Using Anger Control Strategies
- Using Structured Problem-Solving (SODAS)
- Waiting Your Turn

ADVANCED SKILLS
- Accepting Defeat or Loss
- Accepting Help or Assistance
- Accepting Winning Appropriately
- Borrowing from Others
- Caring for Others' Property
- Choosing Appropriate Friends
- Communicating Honestly
- Compromising with Others
- Controlling Emotions
- Controlling Sexually Abusive Impulses toward Others
- Controlling the Impulse to Lie
- Controlling the Impulse to Steal
- Cooperating with Others

Antisocial Personality Disorder (Cont)

- Coping with Anger and Aggression from Others
- Coping with Change
- Coping with Conflict
- Dealing with an Accusation
- Dealing with Boredom
- Dealing with Frustration
- Dealing with Rejection
- Delaying Gratification
- Displaying Effort
- Displaying Sportsmanship
- Expressing Appropriate Affection
- Expressing Feelings Appropriately
- Following Through on Agreements and Contracts
- Interacting Appropriately with Members of the Opposite Sex
- Keeping Property in Its Place
- Making Decisions
- Making New Friends
- Making Restitution (Compensating)
- Negotiating with Others
- Preparing for a Stressful Conversation
- Preventing Trouble with Others
- Problem-Solving a Disagreement
- Responding to Complaints
- Responding to Others' Feelings
- Responding to Others' Humor
- Responding to Teasing
- Self-Correcting Own Behavior
- Self-Reporting Own Behaviors
- Setting Appropriate Boundaries
- Sharing Attention with Others
- Sharing Personal Experiences

- Using Appropriate Humor
- Using Appropriate Language
- Using Relaxation Strategies
- Using Self-Talk or Self-Instruction
- Using Spontaneous Problem-Solving

COMPLEX SKILLS

- Being an Appropriate Role Model
- Being Patient
- Clarifying Values and Beliefs
- Differentiating Friends from Acquaintances
- Displaying Appropriate Control
- Expressing Empathy and Understanding for Others
- Identifying Own Feelings
- Laughing at Oneself
- Maintaining Relationships
- Making Moral and Spiritual Decisions
- Managing Stress
- Recognizing Moods of Others
- Resolving Conflicts
- Seeking Professional Assistance
- Tolerating Differences
- Using Leisure Time
- Using Self-Monitoring and Self-Reflection

Borderline Personality Disorder

Suggested Social Skills Training for Individuals Diagnosed with Borderline Personality Disorder

BASIC SKILLS

- Accepting Criticism or a Consequence
- Accepting "No" for an Answer
- Disagreeing Appropriately
- Following Instructions
- Showing Respect
- Showing Sensitivity to Others

INTERMEDIATE SKILLS

- Accepting Apologies from Others
- Accepting Compliments
- Accepting Consequences
- Accepting Decisions of Authority
- Asking for Help
- Being on Time (Promptness)
- Checking In (or Checking Back)
- Choosing Appropriate Words to Say
- Closing a Conversation
- Complying with Reasonable Requests
- Contributing to Discussions (Joining in a Conversation)
- Following Rules
- Getting Another Person's Attention
- Giving Compliments
- Greeting Others
- Initiating a Conversation
- Interrupting Appropriately
- Introducing Others
- Listening to Others
- Maintaining a Conversation
- Maintaining an Appropriate Appearance

- Making an Apology
- Making Positive Self-Statements
- Making Positive Statements about Others
- Offering Assistance or Help
- Participating in Activities
- Refraining from Possessing Contraband or Drugs
- Reporting Emergencies
- Resisting Peer Pressure
- Saying Good-Bye to Guests
- Saying "No" Assertively
- Seeking Positive Attention
- Showing Appreciation
- Using an Appropriate Voice Tone
- Using Anger Control Strategies
- Using Structured Problem-Solving (SODAS)

ADVANCED SKILLS

- Accepting Defeat or Loss
- Accepting Help or Assistance
- Accepting Winning Appropriately
- Advocating for Oneself
- Analyzing Skills Needed for Different Situations
- Analyzing Social Situations
- Choosing Appropriate Friends
- Communicating Honestly
- Compromising with Others
- Controlling Emotions
- Controlling the Impulse to Lie

Borderline Personality Disorder (Cont)

- Cooperating with Others
- Coping with Anger and Aggression from Others
- Coping with Change
- Coping with Conflict
- Coping with Sad Feelings (or Depression)
- Dealing with an Accusation
- Dealing with Boredom
- Dealing with Contradictory Messages
- Dealing with Frustration
- Dealing with Rejection
- Delaying Gratification
- Displaying Effort
- Displaying Sportsmanship
- Expressing Appropriate Affection
- Expressing Feelings Appropriately
- Expressing Optimism
- Following Through on Agreements and Contracts
- Making Decisions
- Making New Friends
- Negotiating with Others
- Preparing for a Stressful Conversation
- Preventing Trouble with Others
- Problem-Solving a Disagreement
- Responding to Complaints
- Responding to Others' Feelings
- Responding to Others' Humor
- Responding to Teasing
- Self-Correcting Own Behavior
- Self-Reporting Own Behaviors
- Setting Appropriate Boundaries
- Sharing Attention with Others

- Sharing Personal Experiences
- Using Relaxation Strategies
- Using Self-Talk or Self-Instruction
- Using Spontaneous Problem-Solving

COMPLEX SKILLS

- Altering One's Environment
- Being an Appropriate Role Model
- Being Patient
- Clarifying Values and Beliefs
- Differentiating Friends from Acquaintances
- Displaying Appropriate Control
- Identifying Own Feelings
- Laughing at Oneself
- Maintaining Relationships
- Managing Stress
- Resolving Conflicts
- Seeking Professional Assistance
- Using Leisure Time
- Using Self-Monitoring and Self-Reflection

Histrionic Personality Disorder

Suggested Social Skills Training for Individuals Diagnosed with Histrionic Personality Disorder

BASIC SKILLS

- Accepting Criticism or a Consequence
- Accepting "No" for an Answer
- Following Instructions
- Showing Respect

INTERMEDIATE SKILLS

- Accepting Consequences
- Accepting Compliments
- Accepting Decisions of Authority
- Choosing Appropriate Words to Say
- Closing a Conversation
- Complying with Reasonable Requests
- Contributing to Discussions (Joining in a Conversation)
- Following Rules
- Getting Another Person's Attention
- Giving Compliments
- Greeting Others
- Initiating a Conversation
- Interrupting Appropriately
- Introducing Others
- Listening to Others
- Maintaining a Conversation
- Maintaining an Appropriate Appearance
- Making an Apology
- Making Positive Statements about Others
- Offering Assistance or Help
- Participating in Activities

- Resisting Peer Pressure
- Saying Good-Bye to Guests
- Saying "No" Assertively
- Seeking Positive Attention
- Showing Appreciation
- Using Structured Problem-Solving (SODAS)
- Waiting Your Turn

ADVANCED SKILLS

- Accepting Defeat or Loss
- Accepting Help or Assistance
- Accepting Winning Appropriately
- Analyzing Skills Needed for Different Situations
- Analyzing Social Situations
- Choosing Appropriate Clothing
- Choosing Appropriate Friends
- Communicating Honestly
- Complying with School Dress Code
- Compromising with Others
- Controlling Emotions
- Cooperating with Others
- Coping with Anger and Aggression from Others
- Coping with Change
- Coping with Conflict
- Coping with Sad Feelings (or Depression)
- Dealing with an Accusation
- Dealing with Boredom
- Dealing with Contradictory Messages

Histrionic Personality Disorder (Cont)

- Dealing with Frustration
- Dealing with Rejection
- Delaying Gratification
- Expressing Appropriate Affection
- Expressing Feelings Appropriately
- Following Through on Agreements and Contracts
- Interacting Appropriately with Members of the Opposite Sex
- Making Decisions
- Making New Friends
- Negotiating with Others
- Preparing for a Stressful Conversation
- Preventing Trouble with Others
- Problem-Solving a Disagreement
- Responding to Complaints
- Responding to Others' Feelings
- Responding to Others' Humor
- Responding to Teasing
- Self-Correcting Own Behavior
- Self-Reporting Own Behaviors
- Setting Appropriate Boundaries
- Sharing Attention with Others
- Sharing Personal Experiences
- Using Appropriate Humor
- Using Appropriate Language
- Using Relaxation Strategies
- Using Self-Talk or Self-Instruction
- Using Spontaneous Problem-Solving

COMPLEX SKILLS

- Accepting Self
- Being an Appropriate Role Model
- Being Patient
- Clarifying Values and Beliefs
- Differentiating Friends from Acquaintances
- Displaying Appropriate Control
- Expressing Empathy and Understanding for Others
- Identifying Own Feelings
- Laughing at Oneself
- Maintaining Relationships
- Making Moral and Spiritual Decisions
- Managing Stress
- Recognizing Moods of Others
- Resolving Conflicts
- Seeking Professional Assistance
- Using Leisure Time
- Using Self-Monitoring and Self-Reflection

Narcissistic Personality Disorder

Suggested Social Skills Training for Individuals Diagnosed with Narcissistic Personality Disorder

BASIC SKILLS

- Accepting Criticism or a Consequence
- Accepting "No" for an Answer
- Disagreeing Appropriately
- Following Instructions
- Showing Respect
- Showing Sensitivity to Others

INTERMEDIATE SKILLS

- Accepting Apologies from Others
- Accepting Compliments
- Accepting Consequences
- Accepting Decisions of Authority
- Asking for Help
- Being on Time (Promptness)
- Checking In (or Checking Back)
- Choosing Appropriate Words to Say
- Closing a Conversation
- Complying with Reasonable Requests
- Contributing to Discussions (Joining in a Conversation)
- Following Rules
- Getting Another Person's Attention
- Giving Compliments
- Greeting Others
- Initiating a Conversation
- Interrupting Appropriately
- Introducing Others
- Listening to Others
- Maintaining a Conversation
- Making an Apology

- Making Positive Statements about Others
- Offering Assistance or Help
- Participating in Activities
- Saying Good-Bye to Guests
- Seeking Positive Attention
- Showing Appreciation
- Using Structured Problem-Solving (SODAS)
- Waiting Your Turn

ADVANCED SKILLS

- Accepting Defeat or Loss
- Accepting Help or Assistance
- Accepting Winning Appropriately
- Analyzing Skills Needed for Different Situations
- Analyzing Social Situations
- Caring for Others' Property
- Choosing Appropriate Clothing
- Choosing Appropriate Friends
- Communicating Honestly
- Compromising with Others
- Controlling Emotions
- Cooperating with Others
- Coping with Anger and Aggression from Others
- Coping with Change
- Coping with Conflict
- Dealing with an Accusation
- Dealing with Boredom
- Dealing with Frustration

Narcissistic Personality Disorder (Cont)

- Dealing with Rejection
- Delaying Gratification
- Displaying Effort
- Displaying Sportsmanship
- Expressing Feelings Appropriately
- Following Through on Agreements and Contracts
- Making Decisions
- Making New Friends
- Negotiating with Others
- Preparing for a Stressful Conversation
- Preventing Trouble with Others
- Problem-Solving a Disagreement
- Responding to Complaints
- Responding to Others' Feelings
- Responding to Others' Humor
- Self-Correcting Own Behavior
- Self-Reporting Own Behaviors
- Sharing Attention with Others
- Sharing Personal Experiences
- Using Relaxation Strategies
- Using Self-Talk or Self-Instruction
- Using Spontaneous Problem-Solving

- Identifying Own Feelings
- Laughing at Oneself
- Maintaining Relationships
- Making Moral and Spiritual Decisions
- Managing Stress
- Recognizing Moods of Others
- Resolving Conflicts
- Seeking Professional Assistance
- Tolerating Differences
- Using Leisure Time
- Using Self-Monitoring and Self-Reflection

COMPLEX SKILLS

- Altering One's Environment
- Being an Appropriate Role Model
- Being Patient
- Clarifying Values and Beliefs
- Differentiating Friends from Acquaintances
- Displaying Appropriate Control
- Expressing Empathy and Understanding for Others

CLUSTER C PERSONALITY DISORDERS

Avoidant Personality Disorder

Suggested Social Skills Training for Individuals Diagnosed with Avoidant Personality Disorder

BASIC SKILLS

- Accepting Criticism or a Consequence
- Disagreeing Appropriately
- Introducing Yourself
- Talking with Others

INTERMEDIATE SKILLS

- Accepting Compliments
- Accepting Consequences
- Asking for Help
- Choosing Appropriate Words to Say
- Closing a Conversation
- Contributing to Discussions (Joining in a Conversation)
- Getting Another Person's Attention
- Giving Compliments
- Greeting Others
- Initiating a Conversation
- Interrupting Appropriately
- Introducing Others
- Listening to Others
- Maintaining a Conversation
- Making Positive Self-Statements
- Making Positive Statements about Others
- Participating in Activities
- Saying Good-Bye to Guests
- Seeking Positive Attention
- Showing Appreciation
- Showing Interest

- Trying New Tasks
- Using Structured Problem-Solving (SODAS)

ADVANCED SKILLS

- Accepting Help or Assistance
- Analyzing Social Situations
- Compromising with Others
- Contributing to Group Activities
- Coping with Change
- Dealing with Rejection
- Expressing Feelings Appropriately
- Expressing Optimism
- Making New Friends
- Responding to Others' Feelings
- Responding to Others' Humor
- Responding to Teasing
- Self-Correcting Own Behavior
- Suggesting an Activity
- Using Relaxation Strategies
- Using Self-Talk or Self-Instruction
- Using Spontaneous Problem-Solving

COMPLEX SKILLS

- Accepting Self
- Asking for Advice
- Expressing Empathy and Understanding for Others
- Identifying Own Feelings
- Maintaining Relationships

121

Avoidant Personality Disorder (Cont)

- Recognizing Moods of Others
- Resolving Conflicts
- Seeking Professional Assistance
- Tolerating Differences
- Using Self-Monitoring and Self-Reflection

Dependent Personality Disorder

Suggested Social Skills Training for Individuals Diagnosed with Dependent Personality Disorder

BASIC SKILLS

- Disagreeing Appropriately
- Introducing Yourself
- Talking with Others

INTERMEDIATE SKILLS

- Accepting Compliments
- Asking for Help
- Closing a Conversation
- Contributing to Discussions (Joining in a Conversation)
- Greeting Others
- Initiating a Conversation
- Introducing Others
- Maintaining a Conversation
- Making Positive Self-Statements
- Participating in Activities
- Saying Good-Bye to Guests
- Trying New Tasks
- Using Structured Problem-Solving (SODAS)

ADVANCED SKILLS

- Advocating for Oneself
- Analyzing Skills Needed for Different Situations
- Analyzing Social Situations
- Contributing to Group Activities
- Coping with Anger and Aggression from Others
- Coping with Change
- Coping with Conflict

- Coping with Sad Feelings (or Depression)
- Dealing with Being Left Out
- Dealing with Boredom
- Dealing with Embarrassing Situations
- Dealing with Failure
- Dealing with Fear
- Dealing with Frustration
- Dealing with Rejection
- Displaying Effort
- Expressing Feelings Appropriately
- Expressing Optimism
- Expressing Pride in Accomplishments
- Making New Friends
- Responding to Teasing
- Self-Correcting Own Behavior
- Setting Appropriate Boundaries
- Using Relaxation Strategies
- Using Self-Talk or Self-Instruction
- Using Spontaneous Problem-Solving

COMPLEX SKILLS

- Accepting Self
- Altering One's Environment
- Asking for Advice
- Being Assertive
- Clarifying Values and Beliefs
- Identifying Own Feelings
- Laughing at Oneself
- Maintaining Relationships
- Managing Stress

Dependent Personality Disorder (Cont)

- Rewarding Yourself
- Seeking Professional Assistance
- Setting Goals
- Taking Risks Appropriately
- Using Self-Monitoring and Self-Reflection

Obsessive-Compulsive Personality Disorder

Suggested Social Skills Training for Individuals Diagnosed with Obsessive-Compulsive Personality Disorder

BASIC SKILLS

- Accepting Criticism or a Consequence
- Accepting "No" for an Answer
- Disagreeing Appropriately
- Talking with Others

INTERMEDIATE SKILLS

- Accepting Consequences
- Accepting Decisions of Authority
- Asking for Help
- Complying with Reasonable Requests
- Contributing to Discussions (Joining in a Conversation)
- Initiating a Conversation
- Interrupting Appropriately
- Listening to Others
- Maintaining a Conversation
- Making Positive Self-Statements
- Participating in Activities
- Saying Good-Bye to Guests
- Saying "No" Assertively
- Trying New Tasks
- Using Structured Problem-Solving (SODAS)

ADVANCED SKILLS

- Accepting Help or Assistance
- Advocating for Oneself
- Analyzing Skills Needed for Different Situations
- Compromising with Others
- Concentrating on a Subject or Task

- Contributing to Group Activities
- Controlling Emotions
- Cooperating with Others
- Coping with Change
- Dealing with Contradictory Messages
- Dealing with Fear
- Dealing with Frustration
- Delaying Gratification
- Expressing Feelings Appropriately
- Expressing Optimism
- Following Through on Agreements and Contracts
- Making Decisions
- Making New Friends
- Negotiating with Others
- Preventing Trouble with Others
- Problem-Solving a Disagreement
- Responding to Complaints
- Responding to Others' Feelings
- Responding to Teasing
- Self-Correcting Own Behavior
- Self-Reporting Own Behaviors
- Suggesting an Activity
- Using Relaxation Strategies
- Using Self-Talk or Self-Instruction
- Using Spontaneous Problem-Solving

COMPLEX SKILLS

- Accepting Self
- Altering One's Environment
- Clarifying Values and Beliefs
- Displaying Appropriate Control

Obsessive-Compulsive Personality Disorder (Cont)

- Identifying Own Feelings
- Laughing at Oneself
- Maintaining Relationships
- Managing Stress
- Resolving Conflicts
- Seeking Professional Assistance
- Using Leisure Time
- Using Self-Monitoring and
  Self-Reflection

PERSONALITY DISORDER, NOT OTHERWISE SPECIFIED

Suggested Social Skills Training for Individuals Diagnosed with Personality Disorder, NOS

- Refer to specific Clusters for social skills based on criteria that client is presenting with.

Chapter 5

Treatment Planning with a Focus on Social Skill Instruction

Treatment planning should be an integral component of the care system in any setting where troubled youth receive treatment. All members of a treatment team should work together in order to design the most effective treatment plans to meet the individual needs of each youth. When treatment plans are individualized, well-thought out, and comprehensive, youth are more likely to experience success during treatment, overcome their problems, and lead more successful, fulfilling lives.

This chapter includes an introduction to the treatment planning process and the elements necessary for creating effective, therapeutic treatment plans. Four realistic treatment plan examples (based on the three scenarios at the beginning of the book) illustrate how the information in the charts presented from Chapter 4 can be applied in the treatment of children diagnosed with a specific mental health disorder. These plans are typical of

129

those used in a family preservation setting, a school setting, a residential family home setting, and a psychiatric setting, and demonstrate treatment planning across various programs. The social skills prescribed as part of each treatment plan are in italicized type.

Treatment Planning Process

Treatment planning is a key component in addressing and successfully treating the symptoms and behaviors associated with mental health disorders. The treatment planning process guides treatment providers as they consider an individual's history, his or her current problems, and how best to deal with and treat those problems. Treatment planning requires a team of treatment providers from various areas of a youth's life to come together and lend their expertise to the process. With a wide range of treatment team members involved, the quality of service provided can be enhanced through unique ideas, perceptions, experience, and specializations.

Most treatment plans are created during a team meeting. In a school setting, a team meeting might include the youth, his or her parents or guardians, the youth's teachers, a special education representative, and any other specialized staff involved in the youth's education (speech pathologist, occupational therapist, school psychologist, behavior interventionist, etc.). When home-based services are being provided, a team meeting might simply include the family consultant and the family. In a residential care setting, a team meeting might include the youth, his or her parents or guardians, youth care supervisors, youth care workers, and other individuals involved in the youth's treatment (psychiatrist, psychologist, therapist, caseworker, guardian ad litem, probation officer, etc.).

During a meeting, team members discuss and identify the youth's past and current behavior and symptoms to target for treatment. Based on present issues and problems, the team determines the most appropriate goals for an individual youth. The result of the team meeting is a document called a treatment plan.

Several necessary components are included in all treatment plans. First, it's important to include a youth's demographic and historical information. This can include age, gender, race, referral concerns, contact information, insurance numbers, medical history, psychiatric history, developmental history, social history, family history, chemical dependency issues, risk factors (suicidality, homicidality, abuse, etc.), educational history, occupational history (if applicable), and other relevant information. Second, the individual's mental health disorder diagnosis should be stated, which is typically done in the form of the DSM-IV-TR diagnostic axes discussed in Chapter 1. Third, the youth's treatment goals (and how social skill instruction can help achieve them) should be specifically stated. Fourth, the objectives for meeting the treatment goals should be clearly defined so that anyone reading the objectives can understand how they relate to the goals, how to measure them, and what progress is anticipated. Fifth, a youth's progress toward his or her treatment goals since the previous treatment plan should be specifically stated. (This component would not be included if this is the youth's first treatment plan.) Finally, future dates to review progress should be determined and listed in the treatment plan.

Once an individualized treatment plan is complete, it serves as a guide for everyone who works with the youth. It helps ensure that all members of the treatment team are working toward the same goals, provides a method of accountability for the team, and offers a standard against which progress can be measured. A treatment plan should be thought of as a "living" document because it can be modified and further developed at each team meeting, depending on a youth's progress. New objectives and goals can be added when needed, while old goals that have been achieved can be removed. An individualized treatment plan is the best way to guarantee that services from treatment providers are consistent, effective, and, ultimately, successful.

Using Treatment Plans

Good treatment plans are organized, goal-directed, functional, and fluid. They allow treatment to be provided in a systematic, planned, and focused way, while also providing for flexibility based on the changing climate in a youth's environment. Once a treatment plan is developed, it is important for all involved to understand, follow, and use the plan throughout the course of a youth's treatment.

Developing a quality treatment plan isn't easy; it requires time and effort to do it right. Sometimes, treatment providers can get bogged down in the required paperwork and the treatment planning process becomes an exercise in simply filling out forms. When the process isn't taken seriously, neither is the resulting treatment plan. That's why it's important for treatment providers to be diligent as they build an effective, comprehensive plan and follow through to ensure that it benefits the youth.

Remember that a treatment plan is a "living" document. This means it can change as the situation warrants. If, after a reasonable amount of time and evaluation, parts of a treatment plan aren't working, it should be adjusted and changed so that it can better meet the youth's needs.

The treatment planning process helps to ensure that youth are receiving treatment that is focused on their specific problems and associated skill deficits. In addition, individual considerations (developmental level, social influences, cultural norms, etc.) should be reflected throughout the treatment plan. By using individualized treatment plans like those presented here, caregivers can provide quality, effective treatment and increase the likelihood that youth will get better.

Example 1 – 'Hyper' Harry

Synopsis: Harry is an eleven-year-old boy who a licensed mental health professional has evaluated and diagnosed as having Attention-Deficit/Hyperactivity Disorder (ADHD). Symptoms, present since age five, are causing Harry significant problems in school and at home. The diagnosis was based on multiple sources of information including clinically elevated DISC scores for ADHD; clinically significant scores on the BASC Parent Rating Scale, BASC Teacher Rating Scale, and BASC Self Report of Personality on the Inattention/Hyperactivity Scale; a school observation where Harry was found to be off task eighty percent of the time; and biological parent and teacher reports of the following DSM-IV-TR diagnostic criteria:

- Has difficulty paying or sustaining attention.
- Fails to follow through with instructions.
- Is unable to concentrate on details, resulting in careless mistakes.
- Doesn't listen when spoken to directly.
- Is easily distracted.
- Regularly loses homework and textbooks.
- Drags out or avoids completion of homework or chores at home.
- Constantly interrupts others and blurts out answers before questions have been completed.
- Doesn't wait his turn.
- Often fidgets with hands and feet and squirms in his chair.
- Often is "on the go" or acts as if "driven by a motor."
- Often has difficulty playing or engaging in leisure activities quietly.

Family Preservation Remedial Services
Individualized Treatment Plan

CLIENT NAME: Harry Smith	**PARENT/LEGAL GUARDIAN NAME & ADDRESS:** Helen & Thomas Smith 1234 5th Ave. Village, ST 12345 **PHONE:** 555-123-4567
DOB: 5-17-XXXX **GENDER:** Male	**RELATIONSHIP TO CHILD:** Biological parents
ADDRESS: 1234 5th Ave. Village, ST 12345 **PHONE:** 555-123-4567	**LPHA NAME AND ADDRESS:** Lisa Todd, M.S., LISW Psychological Health 1234 Happy Dr. Village, ST 12345 **PHONE:** 555-765-4321
COUNTY: Fort	**MEDICAID NUMBER:** 12345678
PROVIDER AGENCY: AAA Agency 1234 W. Townsend, SUITE 1 Village, ST 12345 **PHONE:** 555-789-4567 **FAX #:** 555-789-4568	**REMEDIAL SERVICE PROVIDER:** Kelly O'Connell, M.S.
PROVIDER NUMBER: #1234567	**DATE SUBMITTED:** 8-27-20XX

DIAGNOSIS

Axis I 314.01 Attention-Deficit/Hyperactivity Disorder, combined type
Axis II V71.09 No diagnosis
Axis III None
Axis IV Moderate environmental stressors, including recent move, father currently out of work, and poor academic performance
Axis V GAF: 62 (on admission)/65 (current)

MEDICATIONS, IF ANY: 15mg of Adderall XR daily

Collaborative Treatment Planning

Collaboration occurred with mental health provider via letter received on 8-23-20XX.

Lisa Todd conducted the mental health assessment on 5-24-20XX and updated the order to include individual units on 8-23-20XX. AAA Agency received the order on 8-23-20XX at 1:38 p.m. The report identified the current target symptoms for Harry as difficulty remaining on task, difficulty completing homework and tasks, difficulty following instructions, and frequently blurting out and making noises. The mental health provider requested that the focus for Harry's remedial services include: increasing time on task, increasing homework and task completion, increasing instruction following, and decreasing blurting out and noises.

Collaboration occurred with Helen and Thomas Smith on 8-17-20XX.

Helen and Thomas expressed their desire to continue with services as they feel it has helped Harry improve his behaviors and also has helped hold him accountable. Thomas reports that the services have helped to improve his relationship with his son. Helen identified Harry's positive attitude as a strength, and Thomas identified Harry's interest in sports as a strength. Harry's parents' primary concern is his difficulty with following instructions. Helen and Thomas feel that Harry needs continued work on improving his ability to follow instructions promptly after they are given and remaining on task until the task is completed.

Collaboration occurred with Harry Smith on 8-17-20XX.

Harry is an 11-year-old healthy, Caucasian male. Harry states that he feels his ability to maintain attention has improved since he recently began taking his new medication. However, he thinks he still needs some work on getting tasks done in a prompt and efficient manner, particularly homework. He reports that he is pleased that he is getting along better with his father, and is enjoying spending time with his father once again. He stated, "Dad is on my case less often when I just get things done." Harry also feels that he needs to continue working on using self-monitoring skills. Harry feels that when he does not monitor his behavior, he tends to blurt out more often and do things "without thinking."

Baseline:

Harry follows 40% of instructions given on an average day.
Harry completes homework an average of 1 out of 5 school days.
Harry completes 60% of tasks.
Harry is on task 20% of the time on an average day.
Harry blurts out and makes unsolicited noises about 20 times a day.

Discharge Plan:

Harry will increase instructions followed to at least 70% on average.
Harry will complete homework 5 out of 5 school days.
Harry will complete 90% of tasks.
Harry will increase his on-task time to at least 70% on average.
Harry will blurt out and make unsolicited noises no more than 5 times a day.

Goals and Objectives of Treatment

Mental Health Diagnosis: Attention-Deficit/Hyperactivity Disorder, combined type
Mental Health Symptoms Identified by the LPHA Requiring Remedial Services: Frequently off task, difficulty completing homework and tasks, difficulty following instructions, and often blurting out and making noises.
Desired Outcome: Harry will be able to use positive social skills to improve his ability to remain on task, complete homework and tasks, follow instructions, and monitor his impulsive behaviors.

GOAL #1: Harry will learn social skills to improve his ability to follow instructions.

> **Objective #1: Harry will improve his ability to follow instructions by showing more often that he can follow an instruction after the first time it is given without arguing. This will be measured by behavior chart, self-report, parental report, and Family Consultant observation by 11-30-20XX.**

Service Activity A (Domains I, F, S): The Family Consultant, Kelly O'Connell, will teach Harry the social skill of *Following Instructions* when instructions are given verbally and generalize the use of this skill to family and school environments.

Service Activity B (Domains I, S): The Family Consultant, Kelly O'Connell, will teach Harry the social skill of *Following Written Instructions* and generalize the use of this skill to the school environment.

Service Activity C (Domains I, F, S): The Family Consultant, Kelly O'Connell, will role-play with Harry the skill of *Following Instructions* and generalize the use of this skill to the family and school environment.

Service Activity D (Domains I): Harry will report to the Family Consultant how often he is able to successfully use the skills of *Following Instructions* (verbally) and *Following Written Instructions* on a weekly basis.

Service Activity E (Domains I, F): The Family Consultant will teach Harry's parents how to praise and reinforce Harry when he follows verbal and written instructions. Harry will earn points and/or praise for instructions followed and will be allowed to cash in points for rewards daily.

Service Activity F (Domains F): Helen and Thomas will track Harry's following-instruction behavior on the daily behavior chart and report to the Family Consultant. **(Non-remedial)**

Service Activity G (Domains F, S): The Family Consultant will teach Helen and Thomas how to obtain daily information from the school regarding Harry's following-instructions performance. **(Non-remedial)**

GOAL #2: Harry will learn positive social skills to increase his time on task and completion of tasks.

Objective #1: Harry will improve his ability to remain on task by showing his intent to be on task without interruption. This will be measured by behavior chart, self-report, parental report, and Family Consultant observation by 11-30-20XX.

Service Activity A (Domains I, F, S, C): The Family Consultant, Kelly O'Connell, will teach Harry the social skill of *Staying on Task* and generalize the use of this skill to the family, school, and community environments.

Service Activity B (Domains I, F, P, S, C): The Family Consultant, Kelly O'Connell, will teach Harry the social skill of *Ignoring Distractions by Others* and generalize the use of this skill across all environments.

Service Activity C (Domains I, F, S, C): The Family Consultant, Kelly O'Connell, will teach Harry the social skill of *Persevering on Tasks and Projects* and generalize the use of this skill to the family, school, and community environments.

Service Activity D (Domains I): Harry will report to the Family Consultant how often he is able to successfully use the skills of *Staying on Task, Ignoring Distractions by Others,* and *Persevering on Tasks and Projects* on a weekly basis.

Service Activity E (Domains I, F): The Family Consultant will teach Harry's parents how to praise and reinforce Harry when he remains on task, ignores distractions by others, and perseveres on tasks and projects. Harry will earn points and/or praise for social skills exhibited and will be allowed to cash in points for rewards daily.

Service Activity F (Domains F): Helen and Thomas will track Harry's on-task behavior on the daily behavior chart and report to the Family Consultant. **(Non-remedial)**

Service Activity G (Domains F, S): The Family Consultant will teach Helen and Thomas how to obtain daily information from the school regarding Harry's on-task behavior. **(Non-remedial)**

Objective #2: Harry will improve his ability to complete tasks by showing an increase in completed assignments and chores. This will be measured by behavior chart, self-report, parental report, and Family Consultant observation by 11-30-20XX.

Service Activity A (Domains I, F, S): The Family Consultant, Kelly O'Connell, will teach Harry the social skill of *Completing Homework* and generalize the use of this skill to the family and school environment.

Service Activity B (Domains I, F, S): The Family Consultant, Kelly O'Connell, will teach Harry the social skill of *Completing Tasks* and generalize the use of this skill to the family and school environments.

Service Activity C (Domains I): Harry will report to the Family Consultant how often he is able to successfully use the skills of *Completing Homework* and *Completing Tasks* on a weekly basis.

Service Activity D (Domains I, F): The Family Consultant will teach Harry's parents how to praise and reinforce Harry when he completes homework and tasks. Harry will earn points and/or praise for social skills exhibited and will be allowed to cash in points for rewards daily.

Service Activity E (Domains F): Helen and Thomas will track Harry's homework and task completion behavior on the daily behavior chart and report to the Family Consultant. **(Non-remedial)**

Service Activity F (Domains F, S): The Family Consultant will teach Helen and Thomas how to obtain daily information from the school regarding Harry's task-completion behavior. **(Non-remedial)**

GOAL #3: Harry will improve his self-monitoring of impulsive behavior.

Objective #1: Harry will learn positive social skills to help him improve control of his impulsive behaviors of blurting out and making noises. This will be measured by self-report, parental report, and Family Consultant observation by 11-30-20XX.

Service Activity A (Domains I, F, P, S, C): The Family Consultant, Kelly O'Connell, will teach Harry the social skill of *Displaying Appropriate Control* and generalize the use of this skill across all environments.

Service Activity B (Domains I, F, P, S, C): The Family Consultant, Kelly O'Connell, will teach Harry the social skill of *Using Self-Monitoring and Self-Reflection* and generalize the use of this skill across all environments.

Service Activity C (Domains I): Harry will report to the Family Consultant how often he is able to successfully use the skills of *Displaying Appropriate Control and Using Self-Monitoring and Self-Reflection* on a weekly basis.

Service Activity D (Domains I, F): The Family Consultant will teach Harry's parents how to praise and reinforce Harry when he displays appropriate control and utilizes self-monitoring. Harry will earn points and/or praise for social skills exhibited and will be allowed to cash in points for rewards daily.

Service Activity E (Domains F): Helen and Thomas will track Harry's impulsive behavior on the daily behavior chart and report to the Family Consultant. **(Non-remedial)**

Service Activity F (Domains F, S): The Family Consultant will teach Helen and Thomas how to obtain daily information from the school regarding Harry's impulsive behavior. **(Non-remedial)**

I-Individual, F-Family, P-Peer, S-School, C-Community

This concludes the Implementation plan.

Individualized Education Plan

NAME: Harry Smith   **ADDRESS:** 1234 5th Ave., Village ST 12345

BIRTH DATE: 05/17/XXXX   **CURRENT GRADE:** 6th   **LAST MDT:** February, 23 20XX

DISABILITY
Other Health Impairment
(OHI; diagnosed with
ADHD, combined type)

SCHOOL
Village South
Elementary School

STATE WARD
☐Yes ☒No

PARENT/GUARDIAN
Helen & Thomas Smith

ADDRESS
1234 5th Ave., Village ST 12345

PHONE
(555) 123-4567

The Parental Rights of Special Education have been reviewed with me and I have received a copy.

_____   _____

parent/guardian initials   date

**The school district has taken necessary actions to ensure
that I understand the proceedings of this IEP conference.**   ☐ Yes ☐ No

---

RESIDENT DISTRICT
Village Public School District

ADDRESS
1234 Lincoln Street
Village, ST 12345

PHONE
(555) 234-5678

CONTACT PERSON   Kathy Wong, Ph.D.   (555) 345-6789

The following participants attended the IEP conference:

NAME	RELATIONSHIP TO STUDENT
Helen Smith	*Mother*
Kathy Wong	*School Psychologist*
Carl Fine	*Principal*
Rhonda Rogers	*Regular Ed. Reading Teacher*
Paula Cleary	*Regular Ed. Mathematics Teacher*
Mary Prince	*Regular Ed. Social Studies Teacher*
Latoya Johnson	*Regular Ed. Science Teacher*
Sean Harmon	*Guidance Counselor*
Vince Peters	*Regular Ed. Physical Education Teacher*
Simone Benson	*Regular Ed. Language Arts Teacher*
Olivia Sanchez	*Special Ed. Reading & Lang. Arts Teacher*
Mark Franklin	*Special Ed. Math & Science Teacher*
Collin McKinney	*Special Ed. Social Studies & P.E. Teacher*
Christina Temple	*Special Ed. Paraprofessional*

Present Level of Performance

Include these IEP Team considerations for IEP development:

- The strengths of the student.

- The concerns of the parents/guardian for enhancing the education of the youth.

- For students age 14 and older, consider the student's preferences, needs, interests, and post-school outcomes.

The *Present Level* statements must identify how the student's disability affects involvement and progress in general education.

Family and Student Vision:

Harry's goal for himself is to do well in school. He states that he "would like to get in trouble less often and be able to focus on my schoolwork so that I can do my best." Mr. & Mrs. Smith's goal for Harry is for him to do well in school both behaviorally and academically.

Strengths of the Child and Concerns of the Parents/Guardian for Enhancing Education:

Harry has a good sense of humor. He can be very pleasant and often initiates greetings and conversation with adults and peers. Harry also responds well to praise. He enjoys being the classroom helper and does well when assigned specific tasks. He is a strong reader and comprehends very well. He excels in sports and participates on the school basketball and football teams.

Harry needs to continue to improve his ability to follow instructions. He also needs to improve his on-task behavior and task completion. Harry continues to struggle with talking out and making random noises in class. Due to Harry's disruptive behaviors, he has occasional peer problems.

Harry needs to improve his academic performance across all subject areas. Due to frequent off-task behavior, Harry is not completing in-class assignments. He also is having trouble completing and turning in homework assignments. Harry has difficulty following instructions, which is evidenced by inaccurate completion of in-school work and tests. These behaviors have had a significant and negative effect on Harry's grades.

Present Level of Performance: Harry has difficulty staying focused in class. He often fidgets, daydreams, and blurts out. He has difficulty following instructions, maintaining on-task behavior, and completing work. According to the WIAT-II (Weschler Individual Achievement Test, Second Edition), Harry is functioning at or above grade level in all academic areas. These test scores imply that he is cognitively capable of the work currently being assigned. Currently, Harry is participating in the Boys Town Social Skills Curriculum to remediate his behaviors and allow him to reach his expected potential in the classroom.

Least-Restrictive Environment

Appropriate Education in the Least-Restrictive Environment. Consider accommodation, modification, adaptations, assistive technology, and supplementary aids and services. What does the student require to be successful and to be educated to the maximum extent appropriate with non-disabled peers? What supports do teachers or other personnel need to assist in making this student successful in the classroom?

In the present setting, Harry is able to participate in all general education classes. Harry needs behavioral modifications and accommodations in order to ensure success within this environment. He will be more successful with a small student-to-teacher ratio, use of the Boys Town Social Skills Curriculum, and small-group instruction that can enable him to participate in the regular education classroom. This is currently possible using co-teaching methods. If educational placement should change, this should be reviewed.

Special Considerations:
(check areas that apply and address these in the appropriate areas of the IEP)

- ☒ A. If behavior impedes learning, consideration of appropriate behavioral strategies.
- ☐ B. If English proficiency is limited, consideration of language needs.
- ☐ C. If blind or visually impaired, consideration of need for Braille instruction.
- ☐ D. If deaf or hard of hearing, consideration of the student's communication needs.
- ☐ E. Consideration of student's need for assistive technology service or device.
- ☐ F. Consideration of student's health needs.
  (Attach Related Health Service Plan, if appropriate.)
- ☐ G. Consideration of transition services for students age 14 or older.
  (Attach TRANSITION PLAN.)

Participation in Assessments:

- ☐ The child will participate in district-wide assessments:
  - ☐ without modification
  - ☒ with modification, as specified
    Small group with extended time offered, frequent breaks, and prompts as needed.
- ☐ The child will participate in the alternate assessment.

Participation in Physical Education:

- ☒ This child will participate in regular Physical Education.
- ☐ This child will participate in special Physical Education; see IEP goal(s).
- ☐ This child will participate in a modified Physical Education.

Modified PE Description:

Services/Progress Reporting

Description of Special Education Services: instructional, support, and related services

Service	Time and Frequency	Setting for Services	
Social Skills Curriculum	100%	☒ General Ed	☒ SpEd
Small staff-to-student ratio	100%	☒ General Ed	☒ SpEd
Small-group instruction	As needed	☒ General Ed	☒ SpEd
		☐ General Ed	☐ SpEd
		☐ General Ed	☐ SpEd

*Attached Checklist will detail modifications/accommodations

Description of Special Education Service Delivery:

☐ No   ☒ Yes   Are specialized transportation services required? If yes describe:

Setting Consideration: Consider any potential harmful effects of the selected settings or to the quality of services received.

Options considered:
None noted

REMOVAL FROM GENERAL EDUCATION ___0__ %.

How would providing special education services and activities in the general education classroom impact this student?
Placing Harry in a co-teaching classroom provides the benefits of peer models for appropriate behavior. In a classroom with low student-to-staff ratio and a small population, Harry can get the attention he needs to help him develop the social skills required for success in a regular education classroom.

How would providing special education services and activities in the general education environment impact other students?
Harry's off-task and blurting-out behaviors can distract other students from their studies. His behavioral needs might monopolize the teacher's time. Harry would be disruptive to a regular education classroom that did not offer special education services.

You will be informed of your child's progress __4__ times per year.
You will receive:

☐ An IEP report at least every 90 days.
☒ Updated copies of the goal pages.

An additional page should be used for each goal, and goals for transition services can be recorded on this page.

Baseline: Harry is on task 20% of the time on an average day.

Measurable Annual Goal: By February 20XX, Harry will increase his on-task time to at least 70% on average. Kathy Wong will measure this by no fewer than three, 30-minute time sample behavioral observations during different classes and times of the day.

Short-Term Objectives or Benchmarks

(Each objective or benchmark should be related to enabling the youth to be involved in or progress in the general curriculum, and should be related to meeting each of the youth's other needs.)

1. Harry will use the steps of *Staying on Task* described in the school's Social Skills Curriculum.
2. Harry will use the steps of *Ignoring Distractions by Others* described in the school's Social Skills Curriculum.
3. Harry will use the steps of *Working Independently* described in the school's Social Skills Curriculum.

Progress Report

Schedule	(I) Evaluation Procedures	(II) Progress (date of review)				(III) Is progress sufficient to achieve annual goal?			
Quarterly		Initials	Initials	Initials	Initials	Initials	Initials	Initials	Initials
		Date	Date	Date	Date	Date	Date	Date	Date
		Code	Code	Code	Code	Code	Code	Code	Code

Person(s) responsible for above goal:

Comments on student progress in meeting the goals or objectives/benchmarks:

Statement of how student's progress will be reported to parents (i.e., progress reports, letters, phone calls, etc.):

Progress Report Codes

(I) Evaluation Procedures/Instruments
A. Teacher Observation
B. Written Performance
C. Oral Performance
D. Criterion Reference Test
E. Guardian
F. Parent Report
G. Time Sample
H. Report Card
I. Point Card
J. Other

(II) Progress Measurement
A. Goal Met
B. Progress Made, Goal Not Met
C. Little or No Progress
D. Goal Not Addressed

(III) Is progress sufficient to achieve annual goal?
A. Yes
B. No

143

An additional page should be used for each goal, and goals for transition services can be recorded on this page.

Baseline: Harry completes homework an average of 1 out of 5 school days.

Measurable Annual Goal: By February 20XX, Harry will complete homework 5 out of 5 school days. This will be measured by a daily homework completion report built into the school/home note. Teachers will check "Yes" or "No" for homework completion. This data will be compiled on a weekly basis by Olivia Sanchez.

Short-Term Objectives or Benchmarks
(Each objective or benchmark should be related to enabling the youth to be involved in or progress in the general curriculum, and should be related to meeting each of the youth's other needs.)
1. Harry will use the steps of *Completing Homework* described in the school's Social Skills Curriculum.
2. Harry will write all homework assignments down and use a binder to organize his materials 100% of the time.
3. Harry will use the steps of *Asking for Help* described in the school's Social Skills Curriculum.
4. Harry will use the steps of *Using Study Skills* described in the school's Social Skills Curriculum.

Progress Report

Schedule	(I) Evaluation Procedures	(II) Progress (date of review)				(III) Is progress sufficient to achieve annual goal?			
Quarterly		Initials	Initials	Initials	Initials	Initials	Initials	Initials	Initials
		Date	Date	Date	Date	Date	Date	Date	Date
		Code	Code	Code	Code	Code	Code	Code	Code

Person(s) responsible for above goal:

Comments on student progress in meeting the goals or objectives/benchmarks:

Statement of how student's progress will be reported to parents (i.e., progress reports, letters, phone calls, etc.):

Progress Report Codes

(I) Evaluation Procedures/Instruments
A. Teacher Observation
B. Written Performance
C. Oral Performance
D. Criterion Reference Test
E. Guardian
F. Parent Report
G. Time Sample
H. Report Card
I. Point Card
J. Other

(II) Progress Measurement
A. Goal Met
B. Progress Made, Goal Not Met
C. Little or No Progress
D. Goal Not Addressed

(III) Is progress sufficient to achieve annual goal?
A. Yes
B. No

An additional page should be used for each goal, and goals for transition services can be recorded on this page.

Baseline: Harry completes 60% of tasks.

Measurable Annual Goal: Harry will complete 90% of tasks as measured by his daily behavior report card that is built into the school/home note. Teachers will list ratio of assignments completed (e.g., 4/5). This data will be compiled on a weekly basis by Olivia Sanchez.

Short-Term Objectives or Benchmarks

(Each objective or benchmark should be related to enabling the youth to be involved in or progress in the general curriculum, and should be related to meeting each of the youth's other needs.)

1. Harry will use the steps of *Completing Tasks* described in the school's Social Skills Curriculum.
2. Harry will use the steps of *Checking In (or Checking Back)* described in the school's Social Skills Curriculum.
3. Harry will use the steps of *Persevering on Tasks and Projects* described in the school's Social Skills Curriculum.

Progress Report

Schedule	(I) Evaluation Procedures	(II) Progress (date of review)				(III) Is progress sufficient to achieve annual goal?			
Quarterly		Initials	Initials	Initials	Initials	Initials	Initials	Initials	Initials
		Date	Date	Date	Date	Date	Date	Date	Date
		Code	Code	Code	Code	Code	Code	Code	Code

Person(s) responsible for above goal:

Comments on student progress in meeting the goals or objectives/benchmarks:

Statement of how student's progress will be reported to parents (i.e., progress reports, letters, phone calls, etc.):

Progress Report Codes

(I) Evaluation Procedures/Instruments
  A. Teacher Observation
  B. Written Performance
  C. Oral Performance
  D. Criterion Reference Test
  E. Guardian
  F. Parent Report
  G. Time Sample
  H. Report Card
  I. Point Card
  J. Other

(II) Progress Measurement
  A. Goal Met
  B. Progress Made, Goal Not Met
  C. Little or No Progress
  D. Goal Not Addressed

(III) Is progress sufficient to achieve annual goal?
  A. Yes
  B. No

An additional page should be used for each goal, and goals for transition services can be recorded on this page.

Baseline: Harry follows 40% of instructions given on an average day.

Measurable Annual Goal: Harry will increase instructions followed to at least 70% on average as measured by his daily behavior report card built into the school/home note. Teachers will list the ratio of instructions followed (e.g., 8/10). This data will be compiled weekly by Olivia Sanchez.

Short-Term Objectives or Benchmarks
(Each objective or benchmark should be related to enabling the youth to be involved in or progress in the general curriculum, and should be related to meeting each of the youth's other needs.)
1. Harry will use the steps of *Following Instructions* described in the school's Social Skills Curriculum.
2. Harry will use the steps of *Following Written Instructions* described in the school's Social Skills Curriculum.

Progress Report

Schedule	(I) Evaluation Procedures	(II) Progress (date of review)				(III) Is progress sufficient to achieve annual goal?			
Quarterly		Initials	Initials	Initials	Initials	Initials	Initials	Initials	Initials
		Date	Date	Date	Date	Date	Date	Date	Date
		Code	Code	Code	Code	Code	Code	Code	Code

Person(s) responsible for above goal:

Comments on student progress in meeting the goals or objectives/benchmarks:

Statement of how student's progress will be reported to parents (i.e., progress reports, letters, phone calls, etc.):

Progress Report Codes

(I) Evaluation Procedures/Instruments
- A. Teacher Observation
- B. Written Performance
- C. Oral Performance
- D. Criterion Reference Test
- E. Guardian
- F. Parent Report
- G. Time Sample
- H. Report Card
- I. Point Card
- J. Other

(II) Progress Measurement
- A. Goal Met
- B. Progress Made, Goal Not Met
- C. Little or No Progress
- D. Goal Not Addressed

(III) Is progress sufficient to achieve annual goal?
- A. Yes
- B. No

An additional page should be used for each goal, and goals for transition services can be recorded on this page.

Baseline: Harry blurts out and makes unsolicited noises about 20 times a day.

Measurable Annual Goal: Harry will blurt out and make unsolicited noises no more than 5 times a day. Harry will self-monitor his blurting-out and noise-making behavior by using a written log. The log will be checked by the teacher at the end of each period. At that time, the teacher will mark whether he or she agrees or disagrees with Harry's self-assessment, providing observations if necessary. This data will be compiled by Sean Harman (guidance counselor) and reviewed with Harry on a weekly basis.

Short-Term Objectives or Benchmarks

(Each objective or benchmark should be related to enabling the youth to be involved in or progress in the general curriculum, and should be related to meeting each of the youth's other needs.)

1. Harry will use the steps of Getting Another Person's Attention described in the school's Social Skills Curriculum.
2. Harry will use the steps of *Getting the Teacher's Attention* described in the school's Social Skills Curriculum.
3. Harry will use the steps of Interrupting *Appropriately* described in the school's Social Skills Curriculum.
4. Harry will use the steps of *Self-Correcting Own Behavior* described in the school's Social Skills Curriculum.
5. Harry will use the steps of *Using Self-Monitoring and Self-Reflection* described in the school's Social Skills Curriculum.

Progress Report

Schedule	(I) Evaluation Procedures	(II) Progress (date of review)				(III) Is progress sufficient to achieve annual goal?			
Quarterly		Initials	Initials	Initials	Initials	Initials	Initials	Initials	Initials
		Date	Date	Date	Date	Date	Date	Date	Date
		Code	Code	Code	Code	Code	Code	Code	Code

Person(s) responsible for above goal:

Comments on student progress in meeting the goals or objectives/benchmarks:

Statement of how student's progress will be reported to parents (i.e., progress reports, letters, phone calls, etc.):

Progress Report Codes

(I) Evaluation Procedures/Instruments
A. Teacher Observation
B. Written Performance
C. Oral Performance
D. Criterion Reference Test
E. Guardian
F. Parent Report
G. Time Sample
H. Report Card
I. Point Card
J. Other

(II) Progress Measurement
A. Goal Met
B. Progress Made, Goal Not Met
C. Little or No Progress
D. Goal Not Addressed

(III) Is progress sufficient to achieve annual goal?
A. Yes
B. No

Transition

Harry is only 11 years old and doesn't require a transition plan at this time.

_____ Beginning at age 14 (or younger, if appropriate), updated annually, a statement of the child's transition services, focusing on his/her course of study.

_____

_____

_____

_____ Beginning at age 16 (or younger, if appropriate), updated annually, a statement of needed transition services (indicate the strengths and/or needs for each area):

Instruction: _____

_____

Related Services: _____

_____

Community Experiences: _____

_____

Development of Employment and Other Post-School Options: _____

_____

Daily Living Skills: _____

_____

Functional Vocational Evaluation: _____

_____

Interagency Linkages and Responsibilities: _____

_____

Transition Activities	Agency Responsible	Date

Anticipated graduation date: _____ (must be provided at least 18 months prior to graduation)

Notice of transfer of rights provided:

Transfer of rights will occur at age _____. Date:

Accommodations of Methods and Materials

☒ Provide support and cueing system

☐ Use mnemonic devices

☐ Use visual and graphic representations

☒ Provide written notes and outlines

☒ Highlight important concepts

☒ Repeat key material

☒ Increase hands-on, concrete learning experiences

☐ Use alternative methods of providing information

☒ Break lesson into smaller segments

☐ Allow use of tape recorders or devices

☐ Other_____

Accommodations of Assignments and Assessments

☐ Provide assistance and support in advance

☐ Allow alternate formats and response modes

☒ Provide ongoing coaching and feedback

☐ Allow recorder or word processor

☐ Allow oral responses

☐ Use blocked assignments on worksheets

☒ Divide worksheets into segments

☐ Use folders for storing assignments

☐ Use assistive technology

☐ Use alternatives for written assignments

☐ Increase or decrease the amount of practice

☐ Modify homework assignments

☒ Provide extra time to complete assignments or tests

☒ Break up test administration to shorter sessions

☐ Test orally

☒ Allow writing on test (vs. other sheet)

☐ Other_____

Accommodations to the Learning Environment

☐ Modify the physical setting

☒ Use study carrels or proximity seating

☒ Modify grouping arrangements

☐ Provide guidance and assistance on tasks

☐ Use small-group instruction

☐ Provide peer tutoring

☒ Modify classroom management procedures

☒ Use specialized behavior management procedures

☒ Implement daily or weekly reporting to parents

☒ Use checklists, notebooks, or other on-task aides

☐ Use time-specific assignments

☐ Other_____

☐ NO ACCOMMODATIONS NEEDED

Example 2 – 'Unmanageable' Dwayne

Synopsis: Dwayne is a twelve-year-old boy who has been evaluated by a licensed mental health professional and diagnosed with Oppositional Defiant Disorder (ODD). Symptoms, present for more than a year, are resulting in significant problems at school, home, and in the community. The diagnosis was based on multiple sources of information, including clinically elevated DISC scores for ODD, clinically significant scores on the ASEBA Child Behavior Checklist Parent Form and ASEBA Teacher Report Form on both the Aggressive Behavior syndrome subscale and ODD DSM-oriented subscale, and biological parent and Family-Teacher (primary caregiver) reports of the following DSM-IV-TR diagnostic criteria:

- Often loses his temper.
- Regularly argues with adults.
- Often defies or refuses to comply with adults' requests or rules.
- Blames others for his mistakes and misbehavior.
- Deliberately annoys others and is spiteful and vindictive.

Individualized Treatment Plan
Treatment Family Home Program

NAME: Dwayne Jackson	**REPORT PERIOD FROM:** 3/2/20XX	**TO:** 3/31/20XX
BOYS TOWN ID#: 1234567	**ADMIT DATE.** 2/17/20XX	
MEDICAID ID#: 123-45-6789-10	**GENDER:** Male	
AGE: 12	**DOB:** 01/10/XXXX	**GRADE:** 7th
FAMILY-TEACHERS: Tom & Jane Hopkins	**ADDRESS:** 12345 Farm Circle, City, ST, 68010 **PHONE NUMBER:** 555-123-4567	
LEGAL GUARDIAN: Mark Cobb	**ADDRESS:** 12345 Dodge Street, City, ST, 68111 **PHONE NUMBER:** 555-333-4567	
ATTENDING PHYSICIAN: Dr. Joseph Wright	**THERAPIST:** Carla Peterson, M.S.	
CLINICAL SPECIALIST: Michael Hill	**MOTIVATION SYSTEM:** Daily	

CURRENT DIAGNOSIS

Axis I	313. 81 Oppositional Defiant Disorder
Axis II	V71.09 No diagnosis
Axis II	Asthma
Axis II	Moderate-to-severe environmental stressors: Early physical abuse and neglect, multiple out-of-home placements, ward of the state of Nebraska, uninvolved biological father
Axis II	GAF=53 (current)

Treatment Progress/Update

GOAL #1: Dwayne will learn to respect authority in all environments, including home and school.

Obj. #	Objective	Estimated Target Date	Open/ Closed	Level of Progress			
				A	P	MP	NP
1.1	Dwayne will learn the skill of *Accepting Criticism* by earning fewer than "2" concerns daily.	6/1/20XX	OPEN		X		
1.2	Dwayne will learn the skill of *Accepting Decisions of Authority* by earning "1" or fewer concerns daily.	6/1/20XX	OPEN		X		
1.3	Dwayne will *Follow Rules* at school, earning fewer than "2" concerns daily and "0" homework concerns.	6/1/20XX	OPEN		X		

KEY: Denotes Level of Progress on Objective: **A**=Achieved/Generalized; **P**=Progress Made; **MP**=Minimal Progress Made; **NP**=No Progress

Current Review Period:_____3/2/20XX_____ To_____3/31/20XX_____

In regard to learning to respect authority, Dwayne has made progress in all of his objectives. Dwayne regularly accepts criticism/feedback from Family-Teachers, schoolteachers, and peers. Dwayne earned concerns for accepting criticism/feedback on 3/7, 3/13, 3/15, 3/21, 3/22, and 3/29. Dwayne has complained, rolled his eyes, argued, and made noises instead of accepting criticism/feedback.

Dwayne continues to show progress with accepting decisions by not arguing. He earned concerns on 3/8, 3/11, 3/15, 3/16, and 3/24. The majority of these were for not completing his chores and doing his laundry.

Dwayne has been able to follow the rules at school. He has not earned an office referral and has been able to earn less than "2" concerns each day with the exception of one day. Dwayne struggled in class on 3/18. He interrupted his teacher and spoke out of turn. He received an office referral warning for disrupting the class. Dwayne showed acceptance by decreasing his disruptive behavior and not arguing.

GOAL #2: Dwayne will develop his communication and interaction skills.

Obj. #	Objective	Estimated Target Date	Open/ Closed	Level of Progress			
				A	P	MP	NP
2.1	Dwayne will learn the skill of *Using an Appropriate Voice Tone* when interacting with others, earning "1" or fewer negative consequences per day.	8/1/20XX	OPEN			X	
2.2	Dwayne will learn to engage in appropriate conversations with his peers, earning at least "1" positive daily for using the skill of *Choosing Appropriate Words to Say*.	8/1/20XX	OPEN			X	

KEY: Denotes Level of Progress on Objective: **A**=Achieved/Generalized; **P**=Progress Made; **MP**=Minimal Progress Made; **NP**=No Progress

Current Review Period:_____3/2/20XX_____ To_____3/31/20XX_____

Dwayne has displayed minimal progress in using an appropriate voice tone and volume. He earned concerns on 3/12 for laughing at his peers and speaking over them. On 3/13, Dwayne used sarcastic voice tones when speaking to his peers. On 3/17, Dwayne earned concerns for blurting out answers and yelling in the house. On 3/29, Dwayne used a rude voice tone with both his peers and adults.

Dwayne has displayed improvements in choosing appropriate words to say during conversations with others. He struggles with maintaining a conversation, making positive comments, and not interrupting. Dwayne earned concerns for inappropriate topics and rude language in conversations on 3/3, 3/7, 3/13, 3/16, 3/17, 3/18, 3/22, 3/23, 3/24, and 3/29.

GOAL #3: Dwayne will learn to manage his feelings and emotions appropriately.

Obj. #	Objective	Estimated Target Date	Open/ Closed	Level of Progress			
				A	P	MP	NP
3.1	Dwayne will learn the skill of *Using Anger Control Strategies*, earning one positive per day.	5/1/20XX	OPEN			X	
3.2	Dwayne will use his self-control skills when *Dealing with Frustration*, earning "1" or fewer consequences per day.	5/1/20XX	OPEN		X		
3.3	Dwayne will learn the skill of *Expressing Feelings Appropriately*, earning one positive per day.	5/1/20XX	OPEN			X	

KEY: Denotes Level of Progress on Objective: **A**=Achieved/Generalized; **P**=Progress Made; **MP**=Minimal Progress Made; **NP**=No Progress

Current Review Period: _____3/2/20XX_____ To_____3/31/20XX_____

Concerning the skill of Using Anger Control Strategies, Dwayne has made minimal progress. Dwayne earned positives for using this skill only 10 out of 30 days: 3/5, 3/7, 3/11, 3/13, 3/15, 3/18, 3/20, 3/21, 3/22, and 3/31. On other occasions, he typically chooses to "shut down" rather than use his anger control strategies.

Dwayne has made progress in using the skill of Dealing with Frustrations by having one instance of crying on 3/4. This was brought on by a last-minute notification that his mother would not be visiting him on a weekend as planned. He has had no incidents of aggression.

Dwayne has made minimal progress with expressing his feelings appropriately. He was able to express his feelings about his mother not making family therapy, not being able to participate in Boy Scouts, and his sister not calling for a few weeks. After Dwayne expressed his feelings, he quickly moved on. When he was disappointed about not seeing his mother on the weekend, he wrote her a letter. When he found out he couldn't participate in Boy Scouts, he decided to make some new friends, and he has become active by participating in community functions, playing outside, initiating games, and getting involved in school activities. When his sister was on vacation, he was able to write her a card and then go outside to play. While these are healthy coping strategies, Dwayne also needs to continue working on verbally expressing his feelings to others.

Non-Prioritized Goals

Goal #	Goal Description	Level of Progress			
		A	P	MP	NP
4	Dwayne will learn independent living skills.		X		
5	Dwayne will improve his relationships with his family.		X		
6	Dwayne will develop his academic skills.		X		

In regard to Dwayne's non-prioritized goals, he has made progress in all areas. Dwayne has improved his hygiene by showering, brushing his teeth, and cleaning his room on a daily basis. He also has participated in the self-government process in the home by being elected manager of the home by his peers.

Dwayne has made efforts to improve his relationship with both his mother and his caseworker. He has been able to work on his relationship with his caseworker, Tonya, by speaking to her on a regular basis and sending her letters bi-weekly. Dwayne has discussed his progress with his mother and continues to ask how she is doing.

Academically, Dwayne was able to participate in class on a regular basis. Dwayne's teachers reported that he was pleasant to have in class and that he displayed good quality work on his assignments. Dwayne finished the fourth quarter with a 3.0 GPA. Dwayne did not miss a day of school, earning only 2 tardies for the semester.

TREATMENT STRATEGIES: Family-Teachers will target social skills in areas where Dwayne is deficient. Family-Teachers will do role-plays and complete daily skill review sheets each day. Family-Teachers will make sure that Dwayne has appropriate prosocial activities to engage in with his peers. Family-Teachers will check Dwayne's homework each night for completion and check his organizational skills. Family-Teachers will use the SODAS (Situation, Options, Disadvantages, Advantages, Solution) method with Dwayne to help him solve problems and critically think through important school, peer, and personal issues. Family-Teachers will use self-government meetings to promote accepting and giving feedback, as well as problem solving. Family-Teachers will have Dwayne set daily goals for himself and teach appropriate conversation and friendship skills to Dwayne.

LEGAL AND AGENCY INVOLVEMENT: Dwayne is a state ward. His case manager is Tonya Thompson. She can be reached at 555-321-4567. He also has a guardian ad litem (GAL), Mark Cobb.

ASSESSMENT ACTIVITY: Ongoing academic assessment, therapeutic assessment, medication review, direct observation, in-home observation, weekly consultation, and card reviews will be conducted to assess Dwayne's progress in the Treatment Family Home program.

Responsible Parties (Modalities)					
Medical Professional (as needed)	X	Health Care Coordinator (as needed)		Specialized Religious Education (as needed)	
Psychiatric Professional (monthly)	X	Nutritionist (as needed)		Chemical Dependency Services (as needed)	
Medications (daily as needed)	X	Common Sense Parenting® (weekly)		Other	
Specialized Clinical Services (weekly)	X	Specialized Family Services (as needed)	X		
Specialized Educational Services (daily)	X	Treatment Family Home Program (daily)	X		

Medical Information	
CURRENT MEDICATIONS: Dwayne is currently off all psychotropic medications.	**PAST MEDICATIONS:** Depakote, DDAVP, Zyprexa, Ferrous Sulphate, Clonidine, Dexedrine, Imipramine, Risperdal
MEDICAL APPOINTMENTS/CONSULTATIONS: 3/12/20XX - Dental with Dr. Mayer (sealants needed)	
HEIGHT: 65 inches	**WEIGHT:** 109
LAST PHYSICAL/PHYSICIAN: 1/6/20XX Dr. Robins	**LAST DENTAL/DENTIST:** 3/12/20XX Dr. Mayer
MENTAL HEALTH APPOINTMENTS/CONSULTATIONS: 3/13/20XX – individual therapy 3/29/20XX – Dwayne had a treatment team meeting with Dr. Wright.	

Family Work	

STRENGTHS: Dwayne's mother has recently become more involved in his life. Currently, she has supervised calls and therapeutic visitation with Dwayne. Contact with Dwayne's father is limited to letter writing, per Dwayne's request. Dwayne also has an older sister, Tanisha, who has been a consistent adult in his life the last few years.

	Goals	Completed	Not Completed	Ongoing
1.	Dwayne and his mother will attend family therapy regularly.			X
2.	Dwayne and his mother will work on communication skills by talking on the phone on a regular basis. This will be monitored by one of the Hopkins' team members.			X
3.	Dwayne will express his feelings about his father, if he receives letters or chooses to write a letter to his father.			X
4.	Dwayne will maintain appropriate contact with his sister, Tanisha Jackson.			X

FAMILY PATHWAY: None/Minimal Contact.

FAMILY CONTACT: 3/11/20XX - Dwayne called his mother on her birthday.
3/11/20XX - Dwayne sent a letter to both his caseworker and his mother.
3/12/20XX - Family therapy cancelled due to transportation conflict.
3/19/20XX - Dwayne sent letters to his mother, his caseworker, and his sister.

FAMILY THERAPY: Dwayne was scheduled for family therapy on 3/12/20XX. Family therapy did not occur due to transportation concerns and his mother not being able to attend the therapy session.

Discharge Plan Review:

REFERRAL BEHAVIORS: Verbal and physical aggression, out of instructional control, poor social skills, poor coping skills, peer relation concerns, arguing, dishonesty, poor hygiene, and low self-esteem.

PROGRESS MADE: Dwayne has been able to make new friends in the community and he interacts by playing games, riding bikes, and hanging out with his friends on a daily basis. Dwayne has shown improvement with decreasing his arguing and by improving his personal hygiene.

ESTIMATED LENGTH OF STAY & DISCHARGE PLAN: Dwayne will remain at Home Campus until treatment goals can be reached, with an anticipated discharge date of January 20XX. Discharge plan is a foster care setting. Permanency plan will likely be the state foster care system.

BARRIERS TO TREATMENT: Dwayne is socially awkward and could struggle with being teased at school. Dwayne has difficulty coping with family issues, and family contact is very limited at this time.

Review Dates	
INITIAL REVIEW:	2/17/20XX-3/1/20XX
REVIEW #2:	3/2/20XX-3/31/20XX
REVIEW #3:	
REVIEW #4:	
REVIEW #5:	
REVIEW #6:	
NEXT REVIEW DATE:	4/30/20XX

How satisfied are you with the progress you have made over this report period?

_____
Youth Signature

Signatures

1. NAME:_____

    TITLE: _____

    DATE: _____

    ☐ Present   ☐ Conf call   ☐ Did not attend

2. NAME:_____

    TITLE: _____

    DATE: _____

    ☐ Present   ☐ Conf call   ☐ Did not attend

3. NAME:_____

    TITLE: _____

    DATE: _____

    ☐ Present   ☐ Conf call   ☐ Did not attend

4. NAME:_____

    TITLE: _____

    DATE: _____

    ☐ Present   ☐ Conf call   ☐ Did not attend

5. NAME:_____

    TITLE: _____

    DATE: _____

    ☐ Present   ☐ Conf call   ☐ Did not attend

6. NAME:_____

    TITLE: _____

    DATE: _____

    ☐ Present   ☐ Conf call   ☐ Did not attend

7. NAME:_____

    TITLE: _____

    DATE: _____

    ☐ Present   ☐ Conf call   ☐ Did not attend

8. NAME:_____

    TITLE: _____

    DATE: _____

    ☐ Present   ☐ Conf call   ☐ Did not attend

I have reviewed the attached treatment plan and approve its contents.

_____   _____

Joseph E. Wright, M.D.   date

Example 3 – 'Down in the Dumps' Jamie

Synopsis: Jamie is a thirteen-year-old girl who has been evaluated by a psychiatrist and diagnosed with Major Depressive Disorder, Recurrent, Severe. Symptoms are resulting in significant problems at school, at home, and with friends. The diagnosis was based on multiple sources of information, including clinically elevated DISC scores for Major Depressive Disorder; clinically significant scores on the ASEBA Child Behavior Checklist Parent Form, ASEBA Teacher Report Form, and ASEBA Youth Report Form on both the Withdrawn/Depressed syndrome subscale and Affective problems DSM-oriented subscale; and biological parent and teacher reports and therapist observation of the following DSM-IV-TR diagnostic criteria:

- Two suicide attempts in the last 12 months.
- Depressed mood most of the day, most every day.
- Diminished interest in daily activities and previously pleasurable activities.
- Significant weight loss.
- Insomnia.
- Feelings of worthlessness.
- Diminished ability to think and concentrate.
- Fatigue and loss of energy.

Intensive Residential Treatment Center
Comprehensive Treatment Plan

NAME: Jamie Jones	D.O.B.: 12/26/1995
MEDICAL RECORD #: 123-4567-89	
Review Dates	
ADMISSION DATE: 10/13/XX	INITIAL TX PLAN: 10/28/XX
REVIEW #1: 11/12/XX	REVIEW #2:
REVIEW #3:	REVIEW #4:
REVIEW #5:	REVIEW #6:
REVIEW #7:	REVIEW #8:
DATE OF NEXT TREATMENT REVIEW: November 27, 20XX	

CURRENT DIAGNOSIS (Updated: 06/09/XX by Joseph Wright, M.D.)

Axis I 1) 296.90 Major Depressive Disorder, Recurrent, Severe, No Psychosis

Axis I 2) 307.42 Insomnia-Maintaining Sleep related to Major Depressive Disorder, Recurrent, Severe, No Psychosis

Axis I 3) History of 296.90 Mood Disorder, NOS

Axis II V71.09 No diagnosis

Axis III None

Axis IV Moderate environmental stressors including several inpatient stays and long-time best friend moved away

Axis V GAF = 35 (current); past year high = 40

ADMISSION MEDICATIONS: Seroquel 25mg in p.m., Prozac 20mg daily, Abilify 10mg daily

STRENGTHS: Jamie is intelligent, attractive, polite, kind, and likable.

IRTC TREATMENT TEAM MEMBERS: Joseph Wright, M.D.; Juan Gonzalez, Program Director; Carla Peterson, M.S., Therapist; Joan Kemp, Educational Therapist; IRTC Nursing Staff; Mike Shaw, IRTC Unit Coordinator; Jackson Sheppard, IRTC Shift Manager; IRTC Behavioral Health Technicians.

Priority Yes	No	Assessment	Date Identified	Problem List
X		X	10/28/XX	1. Depressed and withdrawn (youth presents at time of admission with a flat affect)
X		X	10/28/XX	2. Insomnia
X			10/28/XX	3. Poor coping skills
X			10/28/XX	4. Poor problem-solving skills
X			10/28/XX	5. Difficulty appropriately expressing feelings
X			10/28/XX	6. Difficulty coping with loss
X		X	10/28/XX	7. Suicidal ideations
X			10/28/XX	8. Suicide attempts
X			10/28/XX	9. School attendance problems (refusal to attend)
X			10/28/XX	10. Peer relationship problems (youth identified that her only female friend recently moved away)
X			10/28/XX	11. Inappropriate boundaries (youth will quickly identify female peers as "friends" without consideration and will quickly become attached to male peers)
X		X	10/28/XX	12. Relationship problems within the immediate family (believes older sister is favored by her parents; parents will often criticize Jamie for small mistakes)
X		X	10/28/XX	13. Self-harm behaviors (youth admits to cutting her inner thighs when upset)
X			10/28/XX	14. Refusal to participate in positive activities
X			10/28/XX	15. Decreased academic performance

*Items checked "no" require justification for lack of inclusion in treatment plan.

GOALS AND OBJECTIVES (established at Review #1)

GOAL A: Jamie will learn how to appropriately cope and deal with her emotions and feelings.

Objectives	Review Period											
	1	3	5	7	9	11	13	15	17	19	21	23
1. Jamie will use the skill of *Making Positive Self-Statements* a minimum of 5 times per day by 02/12/XX.	MP											
2. Jamie will use the skill of *Using Structured Problem-Solving* (SODAS) a minimum of 1 time per day by 02/12/XX.	NP											
3. Jamie will use the skill of *Coping with Sad Feelings* (or Depression) a minimum of 5 times per day by 02/12/XX.	NP											
4. Jamie will use the skill of *Expressing Feelings Appropriately* a minimum of 5 times per day by 02/12/XX.	NP											
5. Jamie will use the skill of *Expressing Optimism* a minimum of 5 times per day by 02/12/XX.	MP											

KEY: Denotes Level of Progress on Objective: **A**=Achieved; **P**=Progress Made; **MP**=Minimal Progress Made; **NP**=No Progress; **D**=Discontinue/No Longer Valid; **R**=Revised, **N**=New Objective; **RS**=Restart

GOAL B: Jamie will develop the ability to build positive relationships with others (relationship building).

Objectives	Review Period											
	1	3	5	7	9	11	13	15	17	19	21	23
1. Jamie will learn the skill of *Saying "No" Assertively* to increase appropriate boundaries with both male and female peers, earning no more than 1 negative consequence per week by 02/12/XX.	NP											
2. Jamie will increase her ability to build positive peer relationships. Jamie will learn the skill of *Seeking Positive Attention* from peers a minimum of 4 times per day by 02/12/XX.	MP											
3. Jamie will work on the skill of *Choosing Appropriate Friends* through individual and group therapy, which will help her build appropriate relationships that support positive behavior and build self-esteem. She will provide at least 1 example per session by 02/12/XX.	NP											
4. Jamie will learn the skill of *Making New Friends* through individual and group therapy, which will help her build appropriate relationships that support positive behavior and build self-esteem. She will provide at least 1 example per session by 02/12/XX.	MP											

KEY: Denotes Level of Progress on Objective: **A**=Achieved; **P**=Progress Made; **MP**=Minimal Progress Made; **NP**=No Progress; **D**=Discontinue/ No Longer Valid; **R**=Revised, **N**=New Objective; **RS**=Restart

GOAL C: Jamie will increase participation in positive activities across environments.

Objectives	Review Period											
	1	3	5	7	9	11	13	15	17	19	21	23
1. Jamie will use the skill of *Doing Good Quality Work* across environments, earning no more than 1 negative consequence per week for poor quality work by 02/12/XX.	P											
2. Jamie will use the skill of *Participating in Activities* across environments a minimum of 4 times per day by 02/12/XX.	P											
3. Jamie will use the skill of *Showing Interest* across environments a minimum of 5 times per day by 02/12/XX.	MP											
4. Jamie will use the skill of *Contributing to Group Activities* across environments a minimum of 3 times per day by 02/12/XX.	MP											

KEY: Denotes Level of Progress on Objective: **A**=Achieved; **P**=Progress Made; **MP**=Minimal Progress Made; **NP**=No Progress; **D**=Discontinue/No Longer Valid; **R**=Revised, **N**=New Objective; **RS**=Restart

GOAL D: Jamie will participate in family therapy with her parents and sister to build a reasonable level of connectedness and trust.

Objectives	Review Period											
	1	3	5	7	9	11	13	15	17	19	21	23
1. Jamie will use the skill of *Giving Compliments* with her sister and parents in family therapy at least 3 times per session by 02/12/XX.	NP											
2. Jamie will use the skill of *Maintaining a Conversation* with her parents and sister in family therapy at least 4 times per session by 02/12/XX.	NP											
3. Jamie will use the skill of *Making Positive Statements* about Others in family therapy at least 4 times per session by 02/12/XX.	NP											

KEY: Denotes Level of Progress on Objective: **A**=Achieved; **P**=Progress Made; **MP**=Minimal Progress Made; **NP**=No Progress; **D**=Discontinue/No Longer Valid; **R**=Revised, **N**=New Objective; **RS**=Restart

Initial Treatment Plan Information

Date:_____

GOAL: Youth will undergo initial assessment in noted priority problem areas.

Objectives:

1. Collect baseline data on: Depression and withdrawal
2. Collect baseline data on: Self-harm attempts
3. Collect baseline data on: Suicidal ideation
4. Collect baseline data on: Peer interaction problems
5. Collect baseline data on: Sleep behavior
6. Collect baseline data on: Coping and problem-solving skills
7. Collect baseline data on: School performance and attendance

Restrictions: Jamie will be intensely monitored due to suicidal and self-harm behaviors. This will be assessed on a daily basis by staff and on a weekly basis by Dr. Joseph Wright.

Motivational Level System: Jamie was admitted on Level 1 privileges.

Expectations for Family/Legal Guardian Involvement: Jamie's parents, Bob and Sarah Jones, will attend family therapy two times per month. Jamie's sister, Jenna, will attend family therapy one time per month. Parents will attend monthly treatment team meetings. Family will maintain regular contact with Jamie and the therapist.

Barriers to Treatment: Previous suicide attempts and inpatient placements

Other Therapeutic and Medical Issues: Jamie will participate in individual therapy one time per week, family therapy two times per month, and treatment group therapy a minimum of two times per week. She also will participate in monthly treatment team meetings. Jamie will be able to identify her medications and the side effects.

IRTC Milieu:

Daily
- Psychotropic medications as needed
- Milieu Therapy (PEM)

Weekly
- 30-50 minutes of individual therapy
- 2-3 hours of group therapy
- 6-7 hours of recreational therapy
- A minimum of 20 hours of educational therapy

Other
- _____

Data Collection:

Daily medical chart probes, professional observation, and motivational system card data.

Reason for Continued Care and Estimated Length of Stay: Jamie was referred to the Intensive Residential Treatment Center due to other failed placements at lower levels of care (outpatient therapy, intensive outpatient therapy, and brief inpatient hospitalization). Length of stay will be based on goals achieved and maintained for a minimum of three months.

Contributing Team Members: Carla Peterson, M.S., Therapist
Absent Team Members: None

Date of Next Scheduled Treatment Review: 11/27/XX

Discharge Plan

Estimated Length of Stay from Date of Admission	• 90-120 days
Criteria for Discharge	• Will report a reduction in frequency, duration, and intensity of suicidal ideation. • Will refrain from self-harm behaviors for a minimum of 30 consecutive days. • Will display an increase in ability to utilize social and coping skills. • Will participate actively across the therapeutic milieu.
Next Projected Placement	• Partial hospitalization/Day treatment
Long-Term Placement Plan	• Home with parents, regularly attending psychiatrist and therapist appointments
Barriers to Discharge	• Difficulty maintaining stability at lower levels of care

Projected School Placement Needs:
  Date of Last IEP
  Date of Last MDT
	• Regular education
	• N/A
	• N/A

Transition	• Transitional passes will be conducted, if possible, to the next level of care to ensure a smooth transition.
Psychiatric Consultation	• Jamie would benefit from ongoing psychiatric consultation as long as she is on psychotropic medication or if any changes or discontinuations are considered.
Therapy	• Jamie would benefit from ongoing individual and family therapy.
Medical	• Routine medical intervention and physicals. Jamie will know the medication names, doses, purposes, and side effects.

Comprehensive Treatment Plan Review

Review #1 Date:_____

Behavioral Summary and Data: During the first part of this review period, we saw more suicidal ideation and self-destructive behaviors. Over the last week of the review period, we have seen more stability, though Jamie continues to struggle with utilizing problem-solving and coping skills. She tends to become withdrawn and stare off into space when upset, rather than express feelings. Jamie has endorsed suicidal ideation when speaking with her therapist and Dr. Wright on three separate occasions, resulting in three separate suicide evaluations. Jamie also must continue to focus on appropriate boundaries with male and female peers because she tries to develop friendships too quickly and becomes clingy. She also had difficulty selecting appropriate friends that would help her make positive decisions. She has involved herself in "dating" relationships with male peers. Jamie did admit that on the 13th of this month, she kissed a male peer. Sleep problems continue to be an issue, with Jamie getting up frequently throughout the night and attempting to roam the halls. It appears this is related to poor coping and problem-solving skills. The most destructive self-harm behavior occurred on 11/17/XX, when Jamie learned that one of her "best friends" was "dating" the male peer that she had kissed on the 13th. She began to scratch at her right wrist until it bled, banged her head against the wall, and pulled out some of her hair. A safety hold was required. Jamie refused to attend school on 11/18/XX, stating that she was just too tired and did not feel well. At that time, she was placed in time-out. After time-out, she was able to attend school for the rest of the day. Otherwise, Jamie has shown improvements in school performance. She is earning grades similar to those she earned before her first inpatient hospitalization. It has been noted that her few positive self-statements and expressions of optimism have been related to school performance. She has to occasionally be prompted to put forth effort, but has continued to improve over the month. Finally, only one family therapy session occurred this review period, and Jamie had difficulty exhibiting her skills in that session. She continued to complain about her parents and called her sister several names.

	Baseline Number											
	1	**3**	**5**	**7**	**9**	**11**	**13**	**15**	**17**	**19**	**21**	**23**
Physical Aggression	0											
Attempted Physical Assaults	0											
Physical Assaults - Adults	0											
Physical Assaults - Peers	0											
Seclusions	0											
Suicide Ideation	10											
Self-Destructive Behaviors	6											
Property Destruction	0											
Threatening Behaviors	2											
Time-Outs	2											
Safety Holds	1											

Restrictions: Jamie remains under close monitoring, which is assessed on a weekly basis by Dr. Joseph Wright.

Motivational Level System: Level 1 Privileges, Basics, ITL: Jamie earned an Intensive Treatment Level consequence on 11/17/XX when she engaged in serious self-harm behaviors.

Barriers to Treatment: Jamie has a history of difficulty maintaining stability at lower levels of care.

Additional Goal/Objective and Intervention Information (new goal areas or revisions): Treatment goals were established during this review period to address Major Depressive Disorder and sleep concerns.

Other Therapeutic Issues Noted

Individual Therapy: Jamie's participation in individual therapy has improved as she has begun to participate more actively, complete homework, and bring topics to session.

Family Therapy: Jamie had family therapy with her parents one time during this review period. She frequently complained and was not open to her parents' feedback.

Treatment Group Therapy: Jamie's participation in treatment group therapy has varied from active and appropriate to disinterested and withdrawn.

Recreational Therapy: Jamie is participating in recreational therapy at this time with some prompting.

Current Medications: Prozac 20mg daily

Medication Changes: Seroquel and Abilify were discontinued during this review period.

Psychotropic PRNs: None

Other Medical Information:
- Height and Weight: 5'4"; 101 lbs

Date of Most Recent:
- History and Physical: 10/29/XX
- Dental Exam: see record
- Eye Exam: see record
- Immunizations: see record

Pending Medical Appointments: • None

Family/Legal Guardian Involvement: Jamie's parents participated in this month's treatment team meeting and attended family therapy one time during this review period.

Academic Status:
Review of IEP Goals and Youth Progress: No IEP; Regular Education curriculum at ninth-grade level
Youth Participation: Jamie has had some minor struggles with being on time to school. Once at school, she completes most of her work without incident. Currently, she has completed 98% of her daily tasks. The uncompleted tasks are those missed during the morning and remain to be made up. As time passes, she is becoming more vocal and her participation is improving.

Pending Meeting Dates: None

Reason for Continued Care: Recent suicidal ideation and self-harm behaviors

Review of Discharge Plan and Estimated Length of Stay: 90 to 120 days, lower level of care such as partial hospitalization or a day treatment program

Treatment Team Attendees: Carla Peterson, M.S., Therapist; Jamie Jones, youth; Bob and Sarah Jones, parents

Absent Team Members: None

Date of Next Treatment Review: November 27, 20XX at 10:00 am

cc:

INITIAL TP	Review #1	Review #2	Review #3	Review #4	Review #5	Review #6
dd:						
dt:						

Review #7	Review #8	Review #9	Review #10	Review #11	Review #12	Review #13
dd:						
dt:						

Review #13	Review #14	Review #15	Review #16	Review #17	Review #18	Review #19
dd:						
dt:						

Review #20	Review #21	Review #22	Review #23	Review #24		
dd:						
dt:						

Appendix

Basic Social Skills and Their Steps

Following Instructions

1. Look at the person.
2. Say "Okay."
3. Do what you've been asked right away.
4. Check back.

Accepting "No" for an Answer

1. Look at the person.
2. Say "Okay."
3. Stay calm.
4. If you disagree, ask later.

Talking with Others

1. Look at the person.
2. Use a pleasant voice.
3. Ask questions.
4. Don't interrupt.

Introducing Yourself

1. Look at the person. Smile.

2. Use a pleasant voice.

3. Offer a greeting. Say "Hi, my name is...."

4. Shake the person's hand.

5. When you leave, say "It was nice to meet you."

Accepting Criticism or a Consequence

1. Look at the person.

2. Say "Okay."

3. Don't argue.

Disagreeing Appropriately

1. Look at the person.

2. Use a pleasant voice.

3. Say "I understand how you feel."

4. Tell why you feel differently.

5. Give a reason.

6. Listen to the other person.

Showing Respect

1. Obey a request to stop a negative behavior.

2. Refrain from teasing, threatening, or making fun of others.

3. Allow others to have their privacy.

4. Obtain permission before using another person's property.

5. Do not damage or vandalize public property.

6. Refrain from conning or persuading others into breaking rules.

7. Avoid acting obnoxiously in public.

8. Dress appropriately when in public.

Showing Sensitivity to Others

1. Express interest and concern for others, especially when they are having troubles.

2. Recognize that disabled people deserve the same respect as anyone else.

3. Apologize or make amends for hurting someone's feelings or causing harm.

4. Recognize that people of different races, religions, and backgrounds deserve to be treated the same way you would expect to be treated.

Steps to all of the social skills listed in Chapter 4 can be found in *Teaching Social Skills to Youth, 2nd Ed.,* **Tom Dowd and Jeff Tierney, copyright © 2005, Father Flanagan's Boys' Home, Boys Town, NE: Boys Town Press.**

References

Achenbach, T.M., & Rescorla, L.A. (2001). *Manual for ASEBA School-Age Forms & Profiles*. Burlington, VT: University of Vermont, Research Center for Children, Youth, & Families.

American Psychiatric Association. (1994). *Diagnostic and statistical manual of mental disorders*. (4th ed.). Washington, DC: American Psychiatric Association.

American Psychiatric Association. (2000). *Diagnostic and statistical manual of mental disorders*. (4th ed., text revision). Washington, DC: American Psychiatric Association.

Bellini, S. (2006). *Building social relationships: A systematic approach to teaching social interaction skills to children and adolescents with autism spectrum disorders and other social difficulties*. Shawnee Mission, KS: Autism Asperger Publishing Co.

Boys Town National Research Institute for Child and Family Studies. (2006a, April). *Boys Town residential data summary* (Tech, Rep. No. 011-06). Boys Town, NE: Author.

Boys Town National Research Institute for Child and Family Studies. (2006b). *Lasting results: Five-year follow-up study* [Brochure]. Boys Town, NE: Author.

Conners, C.K. (2008). *Conners' Comprehensive Behavior Rating Scales manual.* Toronto, ON: Multi-Health Systems, Inc.

Dowd, T., & Tierney, J. (2005). *Teaching social skills to youth: A step-by-step guide to 182 basic to complex skills plus helpful teaching techniques* (2nd edition). Boys Town, NE: Boys Town Press.

Fixsen, D.L., Blasé, K.A., Timbers, G.D., & Wolf, M.M. (2001). In search of program implementation: 792 replications of the Teaching Family Model. In G.A. Bernfeld, D.P. Farrington, & A.W. Leschied (Eds.), *Offender rehabilitation in practice: Implementing and evaluating effective programs* (pp. 149-166). New York: John Wiley & Sons Ltd.

Friman, P.C. (1997). Behavioral, family-style residential care for troubled out-of-home adolescents: Recent findings. In J.E. Carr and J. Austin (Eds.), *Handbook of applied behavior analysis* (pp. 187-209). Reno, NV: Context Press.

Gresham, F.M. (1998). *Social skills training: Should we raze, remodel, or rebuild? Behavioral Disorders, 24(1),* 19-25.

Handwerk, M.L., Smith, G.L., Thompson, R., Chmelka, M.B., Howard, B.K., & Daly, D.L. (2008). Psychotropic medication utilization at a group home residential care facility. In C. Newman, C.J. Liberton, K. Kutash, & R.M. Friedman (Eds.), *Proceedings of the 20th Annual Florida Mental Health Institute Research Conference. A system of care for children's mental health: Expanding the research base* (pp. 297-300). Tampa: University of South Florida.

Hays, P.A. (2008). *Addressing cultural complexities in practice: Assessment, diagnosis, and therapy* (2nd edition). Washington, DC: American Psychological Association.

Huefner, J.C., Ringle, J.L., Chmelka, M.B., & Ingram, S.D. (2007). Breaking the cycle of intergenerational abuse: The long-term impact of a residential care program. *Child Abuse & Neglect, 31,* 187-199.

Kingsley, D., Ringle, J.L., Thompson, R.W., Chmelka, B., & Ingram, S. (2008). Cox Proportional Hazards Regression analysis as a modeling technique for informing program improvement: Predicting recidivism in a Boys Town five-year follow-up study. *The Journal of Behavior Analysis of Offender and Victim Treatment and Prevention, 1,* 82-97.

Larzelere, R.E., Daly, D.L., Davis, J.L., Chemelka, M.B., & Handwerk, M.L. (2004). Outcome evaluation of Boys Town's family home program. *Education and Treatment of Children, 27(2),* 130-149.

Mash, E.J., & Barkley, R.A. (2007). *Assessment of childhood disorders* (4th edition). New York: The Guildford Press.

Papalia, D.E., Olds, S.W., & Feldman, R.D. (2005). *A child's world: Infancy through adolescence.* New York: McGraw-Hill.

Peter, V.J. (1999). *What makes Boys Town successful.* Boys Town, NE: Boys Town Press.

Raval, V.V., Martini, T.S., & Raval, P.H. (2007). 'Would others think it is okay to express my feelings?' Regulation of anger, sadness, and physical pain in Gujarati children in India. *Social Development, 16(1),* 79-105.

Reynolds, C.R., & Kamphaus, R.W. (2004). *Behavior Assessment System for Children – Second Edition manual.* Circle Pines, MN: American Guidance Service Publishing.

Ringle, J.L., Chmelka, B., Ingram, S., & Huefner, J. (2006, February) *The sixteen-year post-discharge Boys Town study: Positive outcomes for behaviorally and emotionally troubled youth.* Poster presented at the Midwest Symposium for Leadership in Behavior Disorders, Kansas City, MO.

Ringle, J.L., Kingsley, D., Ingram, S., Chmelka, B., & Thompson, R.W. (2007, November). *Using Cox Regression Modeling to predict recidivism for youth departing out-of-home care: Implications for program evaluation and treatment of at-risk youth.* Paper presented at the American Evaluation Conference, Baltimore, MD.

Risley, T.R. (2005). Montrose M. Wolf (1935-2004). *Journal of Applied Behavior Analysis, 38(2),* 279-287.

Roid, G.H. (2003). *Stanford Binet Intelligence Scales* (5th ed.). Itasca, IL: Riverside Publishing.

Shaffer, D., Fisher, M., & Lucas, C. (1997). *National Institute of Mental Health Diagnostic Interview Schedule for Children (Version 4.0) [Computer software].* New York: Division of Child Psychiatry, Columbia University.

Thompson, R.W., Ringle, J.L., & Kingsley, D. (2007, November). *Applying Cox Regression to evaluation of post-treatment studies of the teaching family model.* Paper presented at the Teaching-Family Association 30th Annual Conference, Washington, D.C.

Thompson, R.W., Smith, G.L., Osgood, D.W., Dowd, T.P., Friman, P.C., & Daly, D.L. (1996). Residential care: A study of short- and long-term educational effects. *Children and Youth Services Review, 18,* 221-242.

Walker-Barnes, C.J., & Mason, C.A. (2001). Ethnic differences in the effect of parenting on gang involvement and gang delinquency: A longitudinal, hierarchical linear modeling perspective. *Child Development*, 72, 1814-1831.

Weschsler, D. (1997). *Weschler Adult Intelligence Scale* (3rd ed.). San Antonio, TX: Psychological Corporation.

Weschsler, D. (1999). *Wechsler Abbreviated Scale of Intelligence.* San Antonio, TX: The Psychological Corporation.

Weschsler, D. (2002a). *Wechsler Preschool and Primary Scale of Intelligence* (3rd ed.). San Antonio, TX: Psychological Corporation.

Weschsler, D. (2002b). *Wechsler Individual Achievement Test* (2nd ed.). San Antonio, TX: Psychological Corporation.

Weschsler, D. (2003). *Wechsler Intelligence Scale for Children* (4th ed.). San Antonio, TX: Psychological Corporation.

Wilkinson, G.S., & Robertson, G.L. (2005). *Wide Range Achievement Test* (4th ed.). Lutz, FL: PAR Psychological Assessment.

Wolf, M.M., Kirigin, K.A., Fixsen, D.L., Blasé, K.A., & Braukmann, C.J. (1995). The teaching-family model: A case study in data-based program development and refinement (and dragon wrestling). *Journal of Organizational Behavior Management, 15(1/2),* 11-68.

Woodcock, R.W., McGrew, K.S., & Mather, N. (2001a). *Woodcock-Johnson Tests of Cognitive Abilities* (3rd ed.). Itasca, IL: Riverside Publishing.

Woodcock, R.W., McGrew, K.S., & Mather, N. (2001b). *Woodcock-Johnson Tests of Achievement* (3rd ed.). Itasca, IL: Riverside Publishing.

Index

A

Accepting Apologies from Others, 47, 52, 63, 85, 106, 115, 119

Accepting Compliments, 47, 52, 55, 62-63, 70, 72, 76, 78, 82, 85, 92, 108, 110, 115, 117, 119, 121, 123

Accepting Consequences, 47, 52, 55, 57, 62-63, 65, 70, 97, 100, 102, 104, 108, 110, 112-113, 115, 117, 119, 121, 125

Accepting Criticism or a Consequence, 47, 50, 52, 55, 57, 60, 63, 65, 70, 72, 74, 78, 82-84, 97, 100, 102, 104, 106, 108, 110, 112-113, 115, 117, 119, 121, 125, 151, 172

Accepting Decisions of Authority, 47, 52, 55, 57, 63, 65, 74, 80, 83- 84, 88, 91, 97, 100, 102, 108, 110, 112, 113, 115, 117, 119, 125, 151

Accepting Defeat or Loss, 48, 53, 55, 57, 70, 72, 82, 85, 90, 97, 102, 106, 113, 115, 117, 119

Accepting Help or Assistance, 48, 50, 53, 63, 68, 70, 72, 75, 78, 82, 85, 90, 95, 102, 106, 108, 110, 113, 115, 117, 119, 121, 125

Accepting "No" for an Answer, 23, 31, 47, 52, 55, 57, 68, 70, 83-84, 97, 99-100, 102, 113, 115, 117, 119, 125, 171

Accepting Self, 51, 54, 59, 64-65, 68, 71, 73, 75, 77, 79, 83-84, 86-87, 89-90, 92-96, 101-102, 104, 107, 112, 118, 121, 123, 125

Accepting Winning Appropriately, 48, 53, 55, 57, 82, 113, 115, 117, 119

Achenbach System for Empirically Based Assessment (ASEBA), 13, 150, 158

Achenbach Teacher Report Form (TRF), 13, 150, 158

Achenbach Youth Self-Report Form (YSRF), 13, 150

Acute Stress Disorder, 85-86

Adjustment Disorders, 106-107

Advocating for Oneself, 50, 53, 60, 70, 72, 76, 78, 82, 85, 90, 92, 106, 115, 123, 125

Altering One's Environment, 54, 56, 59, 68, 71, 73-75, 77, 81, 84, 86, 87, 89, 93, 95-96, 98-99, 101, 102, 104-105, 107, 109, 116, 120, 123, 125

American Psychiatric Association, 9, 11

Analyzing Skills Needed for Different Situations, 50, 53, 55, 62-63, 70, 72, 74-76, 80-81, 85, 87, 94-95, 97, 105, 112, 115, 117, 119, 123, 125

Analyzing Social Situations, 53, 55, 57, 62-63, 70, 72, 74, 76, 80, 82, 85, 87, 97, 105, 108, 110, 112, 115, 117, 119, 121, 123

Analyzing Tasks to be Completed, 50, 55

Anorexia Nervosa, 26, 96

Answering the Telephone, 47, 52, 62, 82

Anxiety Disorders, 80, 87

Asking for Advice, 49, 51, 54, 64, 68, 71, 73, 77, 86, 107, 109, 111-112, 121, 123

Asking for Clarification, 50, 52, 97

Asking for Help, 47, 50, 52, 61-63, 65, 68, 70, 72, 74-76, 80-85, 87-88, 90, 93-96, 100, 102, 104, 106, 108, 110, 115, 119, 121, 123, 125, 144

Asking Questions, 47, 50, 52, 62, 70, 75, 82, 88, 90, 106

Asperger's Disorder, 24, 52-54

Assessing Own Abilities, 49, 51, 54, 71, 73-74, 79-80, 89-90, 112

Attention-Deficit/Hyperactivity Disorder (ADHD), 4, 25-27,132-149
social skill training for, 55-56

B

Behavior Assessment System for Children, Second Edition (BASC-2), 13, 132

Being a Consumer, 49

Being an Appropriate Role Model, 58, 64, 68, 98-99, 101, 107, 114, 116, 118, 120

Being Assertive, 49, 54, 56, 58, 62, 64, 68, 73, 77, 79, 83, 86, 92, 98, 101-102, 107, 123

Being on Time (Promptness), 55, 115, 119

Being Patient, 49, 51, 54, 56, 58, 68, 73, 79, 84, 89, 98, 107, 114, 116, 118, 120

Being Prepared for Class, 50, 55

Bipolar Disorders, 78-79

Body Dysmorphic Disorder, 92

Borrowing from Others, 57, 99, 113

Boys Town, 36-37
National Research Institute, 39-40
Social Skill Curriculum, 6, 32-33, 35-36
Teaching Model, 6, 20, 29, 32, 34, 36-40
Treatment Family Home Program, 36-37

Budgeting and Managing Money, 18, 49, 51, 56, 71, 73, 79, 102

C

Caring for Others' Property, 48, 57, 63, 72, 78, 97, 99-100, 113, 119

Caring for Own Belongings, 48, 57, 63, 72, 78, 97, 100

Checking In (or Checking Back), 47, 50, 52, 55, 57, 63, 68, 70, 74-75, 99-100, 113, 115,, 117, 119, 121

Child Behavior Checklist Parent Form (CBCL), 13, 36-37

(A) Child's World: Infancy Through Adolescence, 19

Choosing Appropriate Clothing, 48, 9296, 117, 119

Choosing Appropriate Friends, 48, 57, 63, 68, 82, 99-100, 113, 115, 117, 119, 162

Choosing Appropriate Words to Say, 50, 52, 55, 57, 63, 70, 74, 82, 97, 108, 110, 112-113, 152

Chronic Motor Disorder, 59

Clarifying Values and Beliefs, 58, 68, 73, 77, 79, 86-87, 92, 94, 96, 107, 114, 116, 118, 120, 123, 125

Closing a Conversation, 47, 52, 62-63, 70, 82, 108, 110, 112, 113, 115, 117, 119, 121, 123

Communicating Honestly, 48, 57, 63, 68, 94, 96, 99-100, 102, 106, 113, 115, 117, 119

Completing Homework, 31, 50, 55, 137, 144

Completing Tasks, 47, 50, 55, 70, 72, 88, 137, 145

Complying with Reasonable Requests, 47, 52, 55, 57, 63, 65, 70, 80-81, 83-84, 87-88, 102, 108, 112-113, 115, 117, 119, 125

Complying with School Dress Code, 57, 117

Compromising with Others, 53, 57, 63, 74, 80, 84, 97, 108, 110, 112-113, 115, 117, 119, 121, 125

Concentrating on a Subject or Task, 48, 50, 55, 71, 85, 87, 88, 125

Conduct Disorder, 22, 57-58

Conners' Comprehensive Behavior Rating Scales (CBRS), 13

Contributing to Discussions (Joining in a Conversation), 18, 47, 52, 62-63, 70, 75-76, 78, 82, 85, 88, 100, 104, 106, 108, 110, 112-113, 115, 117, 119, 121, 123, 125

Contributing to Group Activities, 48, 50, 53, 62, 71-72, 75-76, 80, 82, 85, 88, 93, 106, 108, 110, 112, 121, 123, 125, 163

Controlling Eating Habits, 30, 48, 72, 76, 96

Controlling Emotions, 24, 50, 53, 55, 57, 59, 61, 63, 65, 68, 71-72, 74-75, 78, 80-82, 84-85, 87-88, 90-93, 97, 100, 102, 104-106, 113, 115, 117, 119, 125

Controlling Sexually Abusive Impulses toward Others, 57, 85, 113

Controlling the Impulse to Lie, 57, 64, 72, 78, 94, 99, 102, 106, 113, 115

Controlling the Impulse to Steal, 57, 64, 72, 78, 99, 102, 113

Cooperating with Others, 53, 57, 88, 97, 106, 113, 116-117, 119, 125

Coping with Anger and Aggression from Others, 48, 53, 55, 57, 65, 68, 74, 76, 82, 85, 87, 95-97, 100, 105-106, 114, 116-117, 119, 123

Coping with Change, 48, 53, 61, 64-65, 68, 71-72, 74-76, 80, 82, 84-85, 88, 90, 93, 95-96, 108, 110, 112, 114, 116, 117, 119, 121, 123, 125

Coping with Conflict, 48, 53, 55, 57, 59, 64-65, 68, 71-72, 74, 76, 82, 84, 85, 87-88, 90, 93, 95-97, 102, 104-106, 108, 114, 116-117, 119, 123

Coping with Others' Negative Emotions, 90

Coping with Sad Feelings (or Depression), 48, 53, 64-65, 68, 71-72, 74, 76, 78, 82, 85, 87-88, 90, 92-93, 94-96, 102, 104-106, 116-117, 123, 161

Correcting Another Person (or Giving Criticism), 52, 63, 82, 97

D

Dealing with Accusations, 53, 57, 64-65, 68, 72, 78, 87, 97, 99-100, 102, 105, 114, 116-117, 119

Dealing with Being Left Out, 48, 53, 55, 65, 71-72, 76, 82, 87, 94, 97, 105, 123

Dealing with Boredom, 48, 53, 55, 58, 65, 68, 71-72, 76, 78, 84, 87, 94, 97, 100, 104-105, 114, 116-117, 119, 123

Dealing with Contradictory Messages, 48, 53, 74, 87, 91, 97, 105, 108, 116-117, 125

Dealing with Embarrassing Situations, 72, 76, 80, 82, 87, 92-93, 97, 104-106, 123

Dealing with Failure, 48, 50, 53, 55, 71-72, 76, 82, 84, 87, 93, 97, 104-106, 123

Dealing with Fear, 48, 53, 61, 65, 71-72, 76, 80-82, 84-85, 87-88, 90-91, 93, 95, 105-106, 108, 112, 123, 125

Dealing with Frustration, 48, 50, 53, 56, 58-59, 64-65, 68, 71-72, 76, 84-85, 87-88, 90, 93, 97, 100, 102, 104-106, 108, 112, 114, 116, 118-119, 123, 125, 153

Dealing with Group Pressure, 48, 53, 56, 58, 68, 72, 78, 82, 85, 87, 100

Dealing with Rejection, 48, 53, 56, 58-59, 64-65, 71-72, 74, 76, 82, 87, 93-94, 97, 104-105, 108, 110, 112, 114, 116, 118, 120-121, 123

Delaying Gratification, 48, 53, 56, 58, 68, 72, 78, 84, 97, 99-100, 102, 104-105, 114, 116, 118, 120, 125

Delusional Disorder, 74

Depressive Disorders, 76-77

Diagnostic and Statistical Manual of Mental Disorders IV (DSM-IV-TR), 4-6, 9-15, 22, 24, 27, 29, 37-38
And diagnostic assessment, 12-14, 26-27, 43-44, 131, 133, 150, 158
Axis disorders, 10-11, 159-160

Differentiating Friends from Acquaintances, 49, 54, 58, 64, 68, 83, 86, 114, 116, 118, 120

Disagreeing Appropriately, 47, 52, 55, 57, 65, 70, 74, 80, 97, 102, 106, 108, 110, 112-113, 115, 119, 121, 123, 125, 172

Displaying Appropriate Control, 49, 54, 56, 58-59, 61, 64-65, 68, 71, 73, 74, 76, 79-81, 84, 86-87, 89-90, 93, 98-99, 101-102, 104-105, 107, 112, 114, 116, 118, 120, 125, 137-138

Displaying Effort, 48, 50, 53, 56, 58, 60, 62, 71, 72, 76, 80-81, 85, 88, 93, 106, 114, 116, 120, 123

Displaying Sportsmanship, 48, 53, 56, 97, 106, 114, 116, 120

Disruptive Behavior Disorder, 57-58

Dissociative Disorders, 95

Doing Good Quality Work, 26, 47, 50, 55, 70, 72, 88, 163

Dowd, Tom, 33

Down's Syndrome, 26

E

Eating Disorders, 96

Ecological circumstance, 24-25, 33, 35-36

Elimination disorders, 60

Encopresis, 60

Enuresis, 60

Expressing Appropriate Affection, 48, 53, 58, 64, 85, 106, 110, 114, 116, 118

Expressing Empathy and Understanding for Others, 54, 58, 64, 89-90, 101, 111, 114, 118, 120-121

Expressing Feelings Appropriately, 48, 50, 53, 56, 58-62, 64-65, 68, 71, 72, 74-76, 78, 80-82, 84-85, 87-88, 90, 92-97, 100, 102, 104-106, 108, 110, 112, 114, 116, 118, 120-121, 123, 125, 153, 161

Expressing Grief, 54, 64, 73, 77, 90, 107

Expressing Optimism, 53, 60-61, 68, 71, 75-76, 78, 80-81, 85, 87-88, 90-93, 96, 102, 106, 108, 110, 116, 121, 123, 125, 161

Expressing Pride in Accomplishments, 48, 50, 53, 68, 73, 77-78, 82, 85, 92, 96, 104, 106, 123

F

Factitious Disorders, 94

Following Instructions, 5, 47, 50, 52, 55, 57, 70, 100, 102, 113, 115, 117, 119, 136, 146, 171

Following Through on Agreements and Contracts, 50, 53, 58, 64, 73, 78, 100, 104, 114, 116, 118, 125

Following Rules, 47, 57, 68, 72, 78, 99, 100, 102, 113, 115, 117, 119, 151

Following Safety Rules, 48, 56, 58, 60, 68, 71, 73, 78, 100

Following Written Instructions, 50, 55, 136, 146

Formulating Strategies, 51, 80, 104, 107

Fragile X, 26

G

Gambling, pathological, 102-103

Gathering Information, 51, 56

Generalized Anxiety Disorder, 22

Getting Another Person's Attention, 47, 52, 55, 57, 62-63, 65, 70, 75, 82, 88, 94, 100, 110, 112-113, 115, 117, 119, 121, 147

Getting the Teacher's Attention, 47, 50, 52, 55, 62-63, 65, 82, 94, 147

Giving Compliments, 47, 52, 56, 63, 82, 110, 112-113, 115, 117, 119, 121, 163

Giving Instructions, 53, 82

Giving Rationales, 53, 82

Global Assessment of Functioning (GAF) scale, 11

Greeting Others, 47, 52, 57, 62-63, 70, 72, 76, 82, 85, 88, 100, 102, 108, 110, 112-113, 115, 117, 119, 121, 123

H

Hypochondriasis, 91

I

Identifying Own Feelings, 49, 54, 58, 64, 68, 71, 73, 75, 77, 79-80, 83-84, 88-89, 92-96, 98, 101, 104-105, 107, 109, 111-112, 114, 116, 118, 120-121, 123, 126

Ignoring Distractions by Others, 47, 50, 52, 55, 97, 136, 143

Impulse-Control Disorders, 97-98, 105

Initiating a Conversation, 47, 52, 62-63, 70, 75-76, 82, 85, 88, 94, 100, 106, 108, 110, 112-113, 115, 117, 119, 121, 123, 125

Intelligence Quotient (IQ), 13-14

Interacting Appropriately with Members of the Opposite Sex, 114, 118

Interacting Appropriately with the Opposite Sex, 48, 53, 58, 73, 78, 85

Interacting with Others, 72

Intermittent Explosive Disorder, 97-98

Internalizing disorders, 22

Interrupting Appropriately, 47, 52, 55, 57, 63, 72, 82, 88, 97, 108, 110, 112-113, 115, 117, 119, 121, 125, 147

Interviewing for a Job, 49, 51, 71, 73, 83, 109, 112

Intimate Partner Violence (IPV), 39

Introducing Others, 47, 52, 62-63, 70, 82, 108, 110, 112, 113, 115, 117, 119, 121, 123

Introducing Yourself, 47, 52, 62-63, 70, 82, 108, 110, 121, 123, 172

K

Keeping Property in Its Place, 48, 58, 73, 78, 99, 114

Kleptomania, 99

L

Laughing at Oneself, 54, 68, 70, 73, 74, 77, 80, 83-84, 86-87, 89-93, 98, 104, 107, 109, 112, 114, 116, 118, 120, 123, 126

Learning Disorders, 50-51

Learning history, 22, 34

Lending to Others, 48, 53

Listening to Others, 47, 50, 52, 55, 57, 63, 75, 88, 90, 97, 102, 108, 110, 112-113, 115, 117, 119, 121, 125

M

Maintaining a Conversation, 47, 52, 62-63, 70, 74-76, 82, 85, 88, 94, 100, 106, 108, 110, 112-113, 115, 117, 119, 121, 123, 125, 163

Maintaining an Appropriate Appearance, 47, 52, 70, 72, 76, 85, 88, 94, 108, 110, 112, 115, 117

Maintaining Personal Hygiene, 60, 70, 72, 76, 85, 88, 94, 108, 110

Maintaining Relationships, 49, 54, 58, 64, 68, 71, 73, 77, 79, 83-84, 86, 89, 94, 101-102, 104, 107, 109, 111-112, 114, 116, 118, 120-121, 123, 126

Major Depressive Disorder, 4, 22, 158-170

Making a Request (Asking a Favor), 47, 52, 63, 65, 82, 94

Making a Telephone Call, 47, 52, 72, 82

Making an Apology, 47, 57, 63, 97, 99, 102, 113, 115, 117, 119

Making an Appropriate Complaint, 49, 54, 107

Making Decisions, 56, 58, 68, 71, 73, 78, 85, 90, 99-100, 102, 106, 114, 116, 118, 120, 125

Making Moral and Spiritual Decisions, 58, 68, 114, 118, 120

Making New Friends, 48, 53, 58, 62, 64, 73, 77, 83, 85, 94, 106, 108, 110, 112, 114, 116, 118, 120-121, 123, 125, 162

Making Positive Self-Statements, 50, 52, 59-60, 63, 65, 68, 70, 72, 75-76, 78, 80-85, 87-88, 90-93, 94, 96, 102, 104, 106, 108, 110, 115, 121, 123, 125, 161

Making Positive Statements about Others, 52, 57, 63, 82, 106, 108, 110, 113, 115, 117, 119, 121, 163

Making Restitution (Compensating), 53, 58, 64, 68, 90, 97, 99-100, 114

Managing Stress, 51, 54, 59, 61, 65, 71, 73-75, 77, 79-81, 83-84, 86-87, 89-9193, 95-96, 98, 101, 104-105, 107, 114, 116, 118, 120, 123, 126

Managing Time, 56, 71, 73, 102

Mental health disorders
  Identifying, 4-6
  Social skill charts for specific, 43-127
  Social skills training for, 18, 29-41

Mental Retardation, 47-49

Mood Disorders, 24

N

National Institute of Mental Health Diagnostic Interview Schedule for Children (DISC), 12, 132

Negotiating with Others, 53, 58, 64, 98, 106, 114, 116, 118, 120, 125

O

Obsessive-Compulsive Disorder, 84

Offering Assistance or Help, 52, 57, 63, 82, 113, 115, 117, 119

Oppositional Defiant Disorder, 4, 22-24, 150-157
  Social skill training for, 57-58

Organizing Tasks and Activities, 48, 50, 56, 71, 89-90

"Other Health Impairment (OHI)," 2

P

Pain Disorder, 90

Parent Rating Scales (PRS), 13

Parent Response Booklet (P), 13

Participating in Activities, 47, 50, 52, 62-63, 68, 70, 72, 74-76, 80-85, 87-88, 90-93, 95, 100, 104, 106, 108, 110, 112-113, 115, 117, 119, 121, 123, 125, 163

Peer influence, 24-25

Performance deficits, 30-32

Persevering on Tasks and Projects, 48, 50, 56, 71, 89, 98, 136, 145

Personality Disorders
  Antisocial, 113-114
  Avoidant, 121-122
  Borderline, 115-116
  Cluster A, 108-112
  Cluster B, 113-120
  Cluster C, 121-127
  Dependant, 123-124
  Histrionic, 117-118
  Narcissistic, 119-120
  Obsessive-Compulsive, 125-126
  Paranoid, 108-109
  Schizoid, 110-111
  Schizotypal, 112
  Social skills training for, 108-127

Pervasive Developmental Disorders, 52-54

Phobias 81-83

Planning Ahead, 56

Planning Meals, 48, 96

Posttraumatic Stress Disorder, 85-86

Preparing for a Stressful Conversation, 48, 53, 59, 62, 64-65, 68, 71, 80, 83, 85, 93, 95-96, 98, 105-106, 114, 116, 118, 120

Preventing Trouble with Others, 48, 53, 56, 58, 64-65, 68, 74-75, 83, 98, 100, 102, 106, 114, 116, 118, 120, 125

Problem-Solving a Disagreement, 53, 56, 58, 64-65, 68, 83, 93, 96, 98, 105-106, 114, 116, 118, 120, 125

Psychotic Disorder, brief or otherwise,, 75

Pyromania, 100-101

R

Reactive Attachment Disorder, 44-45, 63

Recognizing Moods of Others, 49, 54, 64, 111-112, 114, 118, 120, 122

Refraining from Possessing Contraband or Drugs, 57, 68, 113, 115

Reporting Emergencies, 47, 68, 100, 113, 115

Reporting Other Youths' Behavior (or Peer Reporting), 47, 52, 57, 68, 100, 120-121, 125

Residential group home program, 3, 45

Resisting Peer Pressure, 26, 47, 52, 55, 57, 68, 72, 78, 85, 99, 102-103, 115, 117

Resolving Conflicts, 49, 54, 56, 58, 64, 73, 79, 83, 89-90, 96, 98, 101, 107, 111, 114, 116, 118, 120, 122, 126

Responding to Complaints, 53, 56, 58, 64-65, 83, 90, 98, 102, 106, 108, 114, 116, 118, 120, 125

Responding to Others' Feelings, 53, 58, 62, 64, 89-90, 100, 102, 107, 110, 114, 116, 118,

Responding to Others' Humor, 48, 53, 56, 58, 62, 73, 77, 83, 92, 98, 107, 110, 114, 116, 118, 120-121

Responding to Teasing, 26, 48, 50, 53, 56, 58-60, 62, 65, 71, 73-75, 77, 81, 83-84, 92, 98, 104-105, 107, 109-110, 112, 114, 116, 118, 121, 123, 125

Responding to Written Requests, 50, 56

Rewarding Yourself, 51, 59-62, 65, 69, 72-73, 77, 79-81, 83-84, 86-87, 89, 94, 96, 98, 104, 105, 107, 124

S

Saying Good-Bye to Guests, 47, 52, 63, 70, 72, 76, 82, 88, 108, 110, 112-113, 115, 117, 119, 121, 123, 125

Saying "No" Assertively, 47, 2, 55, 57, 62, 63, 65, 68, 72, 78, 81-82, 85, 97, 100, 102, 106, 113, 115, 117, 125, 162

Schizoaffective Disorder, 72-73

Schizophrenia, 70-71

Seeking Positive Attention, 47, 52, 55, 61, 63, 65, 68, 72, 78, 82, 85, 88, 93, 94, 100, 102, 108, 110, 112-113, 115, 117, 119, 121, 162

Seeking Professional Assistance, 27, 49, 58, 65, 69, 71, 73-75, 77, 79-81, 83-84, 86-87, 89-91, 93, 95-96, 101, 104, 107, 109, 111-112, 114, 116, 118, 120, 122, 124, 126

Selective Mutism, 62

Self-Correcting Own Behavior, 50, 53, 56, 58-59, 61, 64-65, 68, 71, 73-74, 77-78, 83-85, 89-90,

93, 94, 96, 98-100, 102, 104-105, 107, 109-110, 112-114, 116, 118, 120-121, 123, 125, 147

Self-Report of Personality (SRP), 13, 132-133

Self-Report Response Booklet (SR), 13

Self-Reporting Own Behaviors, 48, 53, 58, 60, 64, 65, 68, 71, 73-74, 78, 84-85, 94, 96, 98-100, 102, 104-105, 107, 109, 114, 116, 118, 120, 125

Separation Anxiety Disorder, 61

Setting Appropriate Boundaries, 45, 48, 53, 58, 64, 73, 85, 89-90, 98, 102, 107, 114, 116, 118, 123

Setting Goals, 51, 56, 59-62, 65, 69, 71, 73-74, 77, 79-81, 83-84, 86-87, 93-96, 98-99, 102, 104-105, 107, 124

Sharing Attention with Others, 48, 53, 56, 58, 65, 94, 107, 114, 116, 118, 120

Sharing Personal Experiences, 48, 53, 58, 60, 64, 71, 73-75, 78, 83, 85, 89-91, 107, 109, 112, 114, 116, 118, 120

Showing Appreciation, 47, 52, 57, 62-63, 70, 72, 76, 88, 102, 110, 113, 115, 117, 119, 121

Showing Interest, 52, 57, 62-63, 70, 72, 76, 88, 110, 121, 163, 172

Showing Respect, 52, 55, 57, 63, 70, 97, 99, 100, 102, 113, 115, 117, 119

Showing Sensitivity to Others, 24, 52, 57, 63, 70, 97, 99, 100, 102, 110, 112-113, 115, 119, 173

Skills

advanced, 48, 50, 53-65, 68, 70-100, 102, 104-110, 112-121, 123, 125

basic, 18, 47, 50, 52, 55, 57, 59-63, 65, 68, 70, 72, 74-76, 78, 80-82, 84-85, 87, 88, 90-97, 99-100, 102, 104-106, 108, 110, 112-113, 115, 117, 119, 121, 123, 125

complex, 18, 49, 51, 54, 56, 58-62, 65, 68-71, 73-75, 77, 79-81, 83-84, 86-87, 89-96, 98-99, 101-105, 106, 109, 111-112, 114, 116, 118, 120-126

identifying deficits, 27

intermediate, 47-48, 50, 52-53, 55, 57-63, 65, 68, 70, 72, 74-76, 78, 80-82, 84-85, 87-88, 90-97, 99-100, 102, 104-106, 108, 110, 112-113, 115, 117, 119, 121, 123, 125

learning, 5, 23, 34

practicing, 45

self-help, 32-33

social, 6, 23-24, 34

and mental health disorders, 29-127

deficits, 30-32

teaching, 6, 17-28, 34-40

teaching, 29-41

duration of, 35-36

Somatoform Disorders, 88-89, 93

Stanford-Binet Intelligence Scale, Fifth Edition (SB5), 14

Staying on Task, 5, 47, 50, 55, 72, 78, 102, 136, 143

Stereotypic Movement Disorder, 65

Substance-Related Disorders, 66-69
Suggesting an Activity, 48, 53, 83, 110, 112, 121, 125

T

Taking Risks Appropriately, 54, 56, 61, 62, 64, 73, 77, 79, 81, 83-84, 86-87, 95, 103, 124
Talking to Others, 18, 47, 52, 57, 59, 61-63, 68, 70, 72, 74-76, 78, 80-85, 87-88, 90-93, 94-97, 99, 100, 104-106, 108, 110, 112, 121, 123, 125, 171
Teacher Rating Scales (TRS), 13
Teacher Response Booklet (T), 13
Teaching-Family Model, 36
Teaching Social Skills To Youth, A Step-by-Step Guide to 182 Basic to Complex Skills Plus Helpful Teaching Techniques, 33, 35
TIC Disorders, 59
Tierney, Jeff, 33
Tolerating Differences, 58, 98, 109, 111, 114, 120, 122
Tourette's Disorder, 59
treatment planning, 35-36, 45-46, 129-170
    behavioral and emotional considerations, 22-24
    benchmarks, 144-147
    cultural considerations, 19-21
    developmental considerations,18-19
    discharge plans, 166, 169
    follow-up, 40-41, 157, 165, 167-169
    genetic and biological considerations, 26-28
    goals, 152-156,161-164
    individualizing, 17-28, 134-142, 151-156
    intensive residential treatment center, 3, 159-160, 165
    process, 130-131
    progress reports, 142-143
    skill-based,
        fundamentals of, 33-35
    social considerations, 24-26
    transition, 148-149
    using, 131-132
Trichotillomania, 104
Trying New Tasks, 47, 53, 70, 72, 76, 80-84, 87, 108, 110, 123, 125

U

U.S. Census, 9, 15
Using an Appropriate Voice Tone, 47, 53, 55, 57, 70, 72, 78, 88, 97, 110, 112-113, 115, 152
Using Anger Control Strategies, 48, 53, 55, 57, 63, 65, 72, 74, 78, 88, 90, 97, 102, 106, 113, 115, 153
Using Appropriate Humor, 48, 53, 56, 58, 114, 118
Using Appropriate Language, 48, 58, 98, 114, 118
Using Community Resources, 49, 51, 69, 71, 73, 77

Using Leisure Time, 49, 56, 58, 65, 69, 71, 73, 77, 79, 84, 86, 96, 99, 101, 103-104, 114, 116, 118, 120, 126
Using Relaxation Strategies, 48, 50, 54, 59, 61, 65, 68, 71-72, 74-75, 77, 79-82, 84, 86, 89-91, 93, 95, 96, 98, 104-105, 107, 109-110, 112, 114, 116, 118, 120, 121, 123, 125
Using Self-Monitoring and Self-Reflection, 51, 54, 56, 58, 59, 61-62, 64-65, 69, 71-72, 74, 77, 79-81, 83-84, 86-87, 89-92, 94-96, 98-99, 101, 103-105, 107, 109, 111-112, 114, 116, 118, 120, 122, 124, 126, 137-138, 147
Using Self-Talk or Self-Instruction, 49, 50, 54, 58, 61-62, 64, 71, 73-75, 77, 80- 81, 83-84, 89, 91-94, 96, 98-100, 102, 104-105, 107, 109-110, 112, 114, 116, 118, 120-121
Using Spontaneous Problem-Solving, 54, 56, 58, 65, 68, 71, 73-74, 77, 79-81, 84, 86-87, 89-90, 93-96, 98-100, 102, 105, 107, 109-110, 112, 114, 116-117, 118-119, 120-121, 123, 125
Using Strategies to Find a Job, 18, 49, 51, 71
Using Structured Problem Solving (SODAS), 53, 55, 57, 63, 65, 68, 70, 72, 74, 76, 79-85, 87-88, 90, 93-94, 96-97, 99-100, 102, 104-106, 108, 110, 112-113, 115, 123, 125, 161
Using Study Skills, 50, 56, 144
Using Table Etiquette, 48, 53

V

Volunteering, 53, 63, 82

W

Waiting Your Turn, 48, 53, 55, 63, 97, 113, 117, 119
Weschler Abbreviated Scale of Intelligence (WASI), 14
Weschler Individual Achievement Test, Second Edition (WIAT-II), 14
Weschler Intelligence Scale for Children, Fourth Edition (WISC-IV), 14
Weschler Preschool and Primary Scale of Intelligence, Third Edition (WPPSI-III), 14
Wide Range Achievement Test, Fourth Edition (WRAT-4), 14
Wolf, Montrose, 36
Woodcock-Johnson III Tests of Cognitive Abilities (WJ-III), 14
Working Independently, 50, 56, 71, 73, 89, 94, 143